When *Pleasing* Others Is *Hurting* You

DR. DAVID HAWKINS
The Relationship Doctor

HARVEST HOUSE PUBLISHERS

EUGENE, OREGON

Cover by Koechel Peterson & Associates, Inc., Minneapolis, Minnesota

> This book includes stories in which the author has changed people's names and some details of their situations to protect their privacy.

WHEN PLEASING OTHERS IS HURTING YOU

Copyright © 2004 by David Hawkins
Published by Harvest House Publishers
Eugene, Oregon 97402
www.harvesthousepublishers.com

Library of Congress Cataloging-in-Publication Data

Hawkins, David, 1951-
    When pleasing others is hurting you / David Hawkins.
       p. cm.
    ISBN 978-0-7369-2778-9 (pbk.)
     1. Assertiveness (Psychology)—Religious aspects—Christianity. 2. Christian life. I. Title.
    BV4647.A78H39 2004
    248.4—dc22   2003022199

Printed in the United States of America

11 12 13 14 15 16 17 / VP-MS / 10 9 8 7 6 5 4

Contents

Getting Lost in Your Own Backyard

People get lost every day—in mossy woods, in desert ravines, and in urban alleys. But the focus of this book is on those who get lost in the comfort of their own homes, in familiar everyday activities, in raising a family, working at a job, and being a wife and mother. More importantly, this book is about finding your way to a better relationship with God, with your spouse, and with yourself.

If you were to go hiking in uncharted territory, you would do well to take a compass to ensure that you found your way. Unfortunately, many people attempt to navigate the confusing terrain of relationships without help. They think they know where they are and where they are going, but they may not be aware of the perils along the way that can sidetrack them. They lack the emotional and spiritual guidance that can help them stay true to who God called them to be.

How can a person get lost in familiar surroundings? *When Pleasing Others Is Hurting You* will show you how you can unknowingly stray from the path you had set for yourself. For example, you can ignore your own emotions until you can no longer tell what you are feeling. You can ignore your preferences and eventually forget what is important to you. You may sacrifice your opinions for the opinions of others. You might value the advice of others over your own convictions and the voice of God.

Perhaps at one time you knew what was important in your life and sensed God's calling for you, but very gradually you lost your direction. Bit by bit you gave up small parts of yourself by sacrificing traits that were important to you. You forfeited components of your identity to please someone else. In this sense you not only became lost but also lost important pieces of your personality. This process of losing yourself to win the approval of another person is called codependency.

Codependency Research

Researchers and counselors have studied the phenomenon of codependency for 20 years. They initially linked the condition to alcoholism and discovered that those who are married to alcoholics display some of the same traits as their addicted spouses even though they may have never taken a drink. In fact, people can take on the traits of those around them even in situations where alcohol is not involved. Certain individuals are chameleon-like, changing their needs and desires to fit the circumstances. If such a woman were with a controlling man, she might neglect her own well-being to keep her husband happy. If she had parents who were quarreling and needed peace in the home, she might ignore her needs to meet the demands of the moment in the family.

Codependency and the Scriptures

But are we not supposed to give up our needs to please others? Doesn't the Bible say to "honor one another above yourselves"?

Acknowledgments

Completing a book is a huge project, and many helpful and encouraging hands are involved behind the scenes. I take responsibility for the final product, but my manuscript was improved by many able individuals. I would like to mention a few of them, knowing that I cannot name them all.

I would like to thank the entire "family" at Harvest House Publishers—from the president of the company, Bob Hawkins, to the sales and marketing and editorial staff—for believing in this project and assisting me in creating the best book possible. Working closely with them to see this book to completion was challenging yet affirming, and I am thankful for the opportunity to work with so many wonderful people. Your books do make a difference!

More specifically, my personal editor, Gene Skinner, the guy "assigned to me," has again been actively involved in strengthening the manuscript and encouraging me in my writing. His hand will often go unseen or unrecognized, perhaps even by me. But it is there nonetheless, building, enlivening, making a stronger, more powerful book. His name deserves to be on the cover with mine. Thank you, again, Gene.

I have again been fortunate to have Terry Glaspey, friend, able writer, and editor at Harvest House, as my personal "champion of ideas." He knew, and said, this book needed to be written. Please know, Terry, that your encouragement is special to me.

On a day-to-day basis I must thank Christie and Jim again, who have critically yet tenderly read the manuscript, helping me find ways to enliven my writing and the message of this book. Writing a book is a time-consuming task, and the manuscript needed to be altered and strengthened in many ways. I want you both to know how invaluable your advice and suggestions are to me.

I am fortunate to have many other cheerleaders in my life. A few who have applauded the reluctant artist within are my sons, Joshua and Tyson, and friend, Judy. Thank you for affirming both me and my writing.

Finally, I want to thank the men and women I have worked with professionally (always disguised if used in any way in this book for anonymity) who have taught me the importance of being true to our unique nature. As I watch and listen to your stories I am amazed at your courage to learn new skills, set new boundaries, and search tirelessly for your true nature so that you can rise to new heights. I hope that my counsel has, in some small way, encouraged you to rediscover your true course.

This book is dedicated to the courageous men and women who struggle against the odds to set healthier boundaries that will create for them the life they have been called to live.

(Romans 12:10). Certainly we face tension when applying this scriptural advice. We feel the apparent contradiction and wrestle with it. We worry about thinking too highly of ourselves. Many of us try to lose ourselves for the sake of others and then, feeling exhausted and depleted, feel angry and guilty when we try to replenish ourselves in some meager way. We wonder how this advice could be meant for the overworked individual of the twenty-first century. How do we sacrifice ourselves and appropriately care for ourselves at the same time? Should we ever focus on how well we are doing?

These questions have no easy answers, but we can be sure of this: We must responsibly care for ourselves if we are to responsibly care for others. After all, Christ Himself often pushed away from the needy crowds so that He could rest, pray, and prepare Himself for His ultimate mission.

Yes, we are to consider others above ourselves, watching for ways that we can use our spiritual gifts and resources to meet the needs of others. But we must be *responsibly* considerate. For example, we would be foolish to meet the physical needs of others when they are fully capable and responsible to meet those needs themselves. The apostle Paul, in Galatians 6:2-5, helps us distinguish between the needs that we are to meet ourselves (those that are within our ability to manage) and those that require the help of other people (those burdens that we cannot carry ourselves). We were never meant to enable immaturity or irresponsibility!

Many of us have discovered the hard way that meeting the need of another person is sometimes irresponsible. We must be wise stewards of our own bodies and resources, and we must meet our immediate responsibilities to God, to our family, and to our mission. The gospel does not call us to be workaholics, weary and depressed because we are unrested, overworked, and malnourished—with our brain cells screaming for relief. Many have unwisely suffered in the name of the gospel, only to render themselves utterly ineffective.

We face a great challenge to find this delicate balance between service to others and care for ourselves. This struggle appears to be particularly difficult for women. Therefore, this book is primarily for women who have lost their way, though it will be helpful to men as well. In our culture, and especially in our churches, women are particularly prone to losing their way by focusing too much on other people's needs. Many women who move off course in an attempt to please others eventually disconnect from their true spiritual and emotional nature. One day, they wake up and look in the mirror, surprised to see someone that they do not recognize. They find they have developed a "pleasing personality," one that fears setting limits, enforcing boundaries, or making the choices that could bring joy into their lives.

This book will lead you on an exciting quest for perspective and balance. You will discover the influences that have led you off course and into codependency and pleasing others. You will also find your way back to the path of becoming the person God meant you to be.

Chapter One

Getting Lost Growing Up

*The more you listen
to the voice within you,
the better you will hear
what is sounding outside.*

DAG HAMMERSKJOLD

Nearly half the counseling session had elapsed before I realized that the little girl sitting quietly on the chair in the corner of my office had not said a thing. She was dressed neatly; soft, blond curls fell to her shoulders. She clutched a stuffed animal and watched attentively as I talked with her parents and her brothers.

Once I realized my mistake, I took extra care to include her in the remainder of the session. I was glad I did. Though obviously reluctant to participate, she gave added insight into the way her family functioned.

Throughout the session, Mr. and Mrs. Thompson had seemed content to focus on their "problem child." Their narrow gaze was fixed upon Johnny, a 12-year-old whose behavior had become a source of consternation for his teachers and his family. His younger brother, Jeremy, stirred up almost as much trouble. Compared to the turmoil created by her older brothers, Jessica's behavior was exemplary.

The Thompsons had scheduled the appointment after having a conference with their sons' teachers. It seemed that both boys, but especially Johnny, had been behaving badly of late. Johnny showed up late for school, failed to turn in homework, and disrupted class with his horseplay. A meeting with his teacher and Jeremy's teacher confirmed that both boys were having disturbing problems in school.

The Context

In an initial counseling session, I often try to find the context in which problem behaviors are occurring. Children's behavior never occurs in isolation and always has meaning. In this family, the probable reason for the boys' behavior was obvious. The Thompsons were in the process of separating after a lengthy marriage and several attempts at reconciliation. Both were amicable about the separation, but they were clearly distressed. They had agreed, however, not to let their bickering and imminent separation impact their children. If only it were that easy.

The family impressed me as friendly, engaging, and polite with one another. If anything was unusual about this first session, it was the positive regard each person showed the other family members. I saw no sibling rivalry and heard no harsh words from the parents. The tranquility in my office belied the turmoil in the home.

I asked each person to talk about the impending separation and what it meant to him or her. The boys were nonchalant. "It isn't going to really affect us," Jeremy said.

"It's between them and they'll handle it," Johnny said. "They said we can see them as much as we want."

When I asked Jessica about the separation, her response surprised me.

"I just want Mom and Dad to be okay," she said. "I want them to be happy."

At that point Mrs. Thompson jumped in. "Jessica's our little helper. We can always count on her to make things right. She never causes us any problems."

Jessica's Role

After the session ended and we scheduled a meeting for the following week, I reflected on what I'd learned. Two things stood out. First, although the boys expressed no apparent concern about the separation, their problems at school told the real story. Second, Mrs. Thompson's comments about Jessica made me wonder about the impact such pressure would have on the girl. To her parents, Jessica's role was clear:

- She was their little helper.

- She always made her parents feel better.

- She never caused any problems.

I wondered how these expectations would affect Jessica's development. Would her role in the family become set in stone? Did her parents realize how she was developing and how this behavior might impact her?

Jessica seemed to be taking on the role of "the pleasing personality" while her older brothers acted out the family pain. She seemed intent to make herself invisible, to not cause trouble for her parents. The family had enough trouble, and she was determined not to add to it. She was already taking on many characteristics of codependency, which we will discuss more fully later in this chapter. But first, let's look at another family scenario that can create a pleasing personality.

The Millingers

The Millingers were different from the Thompsons in every way except one: They too were inadvertently raising a child with a pleasing personality. But that is not what brought them into counseling.

The Millingers were a large stepfamily that brought together kids who were "yours, mine, and ours." But they were not the Brady Bunch. They came to counseling because they wanted to merge more effectively. Bringing two families together had generated conflict and tension. They wanted help in creating a happier family.

As I recorded some initial history, I found that Jim Millinger had been married previously and brought two sons into the family. Brenda Millinger was also previously married and brought two daughters to the family. After they married, they had three children of their own, bringing the total to seven.

The Millingers' family constellation defied typical strategies. Because of their history, they actually had three "oldest" children and three "babies." Even completing a geneagram—an outline of a family tree that involves the birth order—was a challenge. But several themes emerged.

Jim Millinger's oldest son was a distant, athletic youth. He had chosen to have little to do with the rest of the family. He obviously did not like the other children and set out to do his own thing. He checked out emotionally and physically. Jim's younger son was somewhat more involved, but he too found ways to be emotionally absent from this family that he did not want to be a part of.

Brenda Millinger's two daughters were much more nurturing and concerned about the welfare of the family. They could both see that unifying this compilation of individuals would take a lot of work. The oldest daughter, Linda, was determined to help the family function. She was obviously the most responsible of all the children. She used her organizational skills and controlling nature for the family's benefit. She commonly helped the other children off to school and made sure the house was clean when her parents came home in the evenings.

During the first session, I watched the family members' disjointed attempts to interact with one another. Of course, simply having six children in the same room (one of the older children had chosen to attend a sports event) was chaotic. Some wanted to dominate the conversation, some wanted to distract, and others wanted to disappear into the cushioned chairs. Linda tried in vain to bring everyone together, to make the family function effectively. She scolded the others for any misbehavior.

Linda's Own Place

As I studied the family, I was reminded of Virginia Satir's groundbreaking study of family roles. In her bestselling book *Peoplemaking*, she notes that each child needs to have a unique and distinct place within the family. In fact, children will go to extremes to create their own place. She found that they will usually take on the role and communication style of the *distracter*, the *placater*, the *computer*, or the *blamer*.

The *distracter* wants to take the focus off anything happening at the moment that may be too intense. The *computer* is disengaged emotionally and handles things matter-of-factly. The *blamer* finds fault with everyone, attacking others and using shame to manipulate them. *Placaters* try to please others. They are the harmonizers, uncomfortable with conflict and tension. They are also the codependents that eventually end up losing their own identity in their marriages and other relationships.[1]

Linda was not the oldest of the seven, but she had decided early on that she could bring the three families together. She wanted harmony, and she hated to see her siblings and parents in pain. Slowly, gradually, she lost track of her own feelings and opinions, and she based every decision on her desire to bring peace to the family.

As I came to know the Millingers, I learned that Linda had always been a sensitive child. She could sense her parent's pain. She watched them closely as they struggled to unite this disjointed group. Bit by bit she set aside her own dreams and goals—her very self— as she tried to make one family out of three. When her parents were busy at work, she supervised the household. When they were too tired to care for the younger children, she became a second mother. When her brothers and sisters got out of hand, Linda did her best to make them behave.

Linda was an astute observer. She noticed the need for a placater in the family. She found a unique role to play, one that offered her self-esteem and a special place in the family structure. She saw that her parents were often exhausted from their jobs and looked to her to care for the younger children. The more she did, the more she demonstrated that she was capable of caring for the family. And the more her parents relied upon her. The stage was set for her to take on a pleasing personality.

For her efforts, Linda was both rewarded and chided. At times the other children liked the attention. She took them to the park to play, helped them pick out clothes for school, and baked them special snacks after school. However, they didn't appreciate her acting as a second mother and disciplining them. They criticized her for being bossy.

Sadly, as I watched the Millingers interact during the counseling session, I saw that Linda had become lost in the family. She was no longer an innocent 14-year-old girl. She was 14 going on 25. The playfulness of youth had disappeared. She spent so much energy protecting, encouraging, and challenging her siblings that she had forgotten to take care of herself. She was lost in the world of codependency.

Codependency

This book is about codependency in families and churches— and how to grow beyond it. These definitions from some of the leaders in the codependency movement will help us understand this important dynamic:

Codependency is the absence of relationship with self, a child's reaction to a dysfunctional family. When children live with people who are not dependable, the child never learns to depend on others or self in healthy ways; they depend on fixes, externals and inappropriate people. They allow people to depend on them, or they isolate and appear independent. Dependency on externals becomes an addiction. Codependency is a symptom of abuse and the loss of identity, which is self-intimacy.[2]

Codependency is a specific condition that is characterized by preoccupation and extreme dependence, emotionally, socially, and sometimes physically on a person or object. Eventually this dependence on another person becomes a pathological condition that affects the codependent and all other relationships.[3]

Codependency is a pattern of living, coping and problem solving created and maintained by a set of dysfunctional rules within the family or social system. These rules interfere with healthy growth and make constructive change very difficult, if not impossible.[4]

Codependency is a dependence of focus on another person, on the relationship at the expense of the self.[5]

These definitions help us understand how Jessica Thompson and Linda Millinger began to lose their own identity because of codependency. We can see how Jessica became lost because her parents were caught up in their own pain. Somehow, inadvertently, Jessica received the message that her own sadness over her parents' separation wasn't as important as her family's other problems. She determined that she had to be the good child and not cause more distress for the family. Her parents, caught up in their own troubles, failed to see that Jessica was becoming overly compliant and sacrificing her own well-being for the sake of the family.

In a different context, Linda noticed her parents struggling to bring two disparate families together. She observed their inability to effectively create one new family. She decided, probably unconsciously, to assist them in the process. She also decided, just as unconsciously, to forgo her own youth and act like an adult in an attempt to help her parents. She doesn't understand the dangerous consequences of these decisions.

Jessica and Linda will lose themselves slowly, quietly. The transition never happens in one fell swoop. The counselor who is assisting families with this type of problem must help restore a healthy balance. This means that parents must behave as parents so that children can be children. Then each person can be unique, happy, and responsible.

Families That Create Codependents

Parents do not intentionally make codependents of their children. No one sets out to abuse, neglect, or create dysfunctional family systems. Yet it happens. We are told in the Scriptures that "the sin of the fathers" will be passed down for generations (Exodus 20:5; 34:7; Numbers 14:18). The weaknesses in our personalities affect the people around us. Families become dysfunctional, and children lose their way. When children are lost to codependency, they often grow up and become lost in their marriages. Fortunately, God lays out His design for families in which children are loved and nurtured and do not carry the burden of becoming codependent by caring for the needs of their parents.

How do families set a child up to become codependent? As you consider what is happening in the Thompson and Millinger homes, perhaps you see some things that concern you. Perhaps you can even identify with them. These families are very typical, but they are dysfunctional in many ways. They are not functioning as effectively as they might under ideal conditions. (Unfortunately, life rarely takes place under ideal conditions!) We see a number of common traits in dysfunctional families that can influence children to develop pleasing personalities that are deeply rooted in codependency.

In the dysfunctional family, children learn that they must set their own dependency needs aside in favor of their parents' needs. While these children may appear to depend upon their parents, in fact the parents depend upon the children to meet their needs. A disturbing role reversal takes place. Children may believe that the parents were "there for them" when, in fact, the children were there for the parents. Terry Kellogg helps us understand how this dysfunctional process takes place.

> Developmentally we first depend on others and then ourselves, thereby being able to do both, which is first called interdependence. A codependent cannot depend on other people or themselves in healthy ways. They also learn not to depend on their feelings as guides in life. Codependents compensate for this by becoming very dependable and having people depend on them...It is the inability to depend, in appropriate ways, on self and others, which sets up the excess dependency on things that become destructive in our lives, our addictions. This addictiveness moves with us through the spectrum of society including family, community, business, church and government. All have become addictive systems.[6]

And so we see that the problem of becoming overly pleasing at our own expense can begin very early in life. No one wants it to happen. But for a variety of reasons—often because of pain occurring in the lives of the parents—it does happen. Children become lost. Even more tragically, as adults their lives become fully dependent on pleasing others.

Unhealthy Boundaries

Just as travelers need boundaries to keep them from getting off course, family members need clear and helpful boundaries to keep them from developing pleasing personalities. Undefined boundaries can cause several problems. The primary culprit is a process of *enmeshment* within the family. Enmeshment occurs when people are not able to identify where their personality ends and another person's begins. For example,

- They do not know what they are responsible for and what is none of their business.

- They are not able to clearly differentiate what they are feeling from the feelings of other family members.

- They are not able to decide for themselves what they want and what other people want for them.

Life can become horrifically confusing for people in families without boundaries.

When children learn to care for other people but not to care for themselves, they begin to define themselves by other people's standards. Instead of deciding what they value, they look to someone else to determine what is important. They are all right if someone— a relative, friend, teacher, or coach—says they are all right. Can you see how disturbing and confusing this would be to a child?

Inappropriate Rules

Children can also develop unhealthy boundaries when they face rigid, dysfunctional family rules. These rules may be overt and clear, or they may be unspoken and fuzzy. In either case, the helpless children learn quickly that they must conform to this unhealthy set of rules in order to receive the love and attention they so desperately need. Consider these oppressive rules that Robert Subby, in his book *Beyond Codependency,* found to exist within the codependent family.

- Don't feel or talk about feelings.

- Don't think.

- Don't identify, talk about, or solve problems.

- Don't be who you are—be good, right, strong, and perfect.

- Don't be selfish—take care of others and neglect yourself.

- Don't have fun—don't be silly or enjoy life.

- Don't trust other people or yourself.

- Don't be vulnerable.

- Don't be direct.

- Don't get close to people.

- Don't grow, change, or do anything to rock this family's boat.[7]

Other Messages

Perhaps even more damaging than these rules are other messages codependents receive. Melodie Beattie has determined that many children grow up with the following beliefs:

- I'm not lovable.

- I don't deserve good things.

- I'll never succeed.[8]

Tragically, children may subconsciously buy in to these beliefs. They are not aware that they are swallowing them or that their parents are unwittingly passing them along. No one can see these beliefs, so no one challenges them. Healing can take place when families bring these beliefs to the surface.

Linda's Boundaries

Let's consider Linda's challenge. Her parents are valiantly trying to combine three distinct families with different histories and different values. They are struggling to make this marriage and family work. They need help and are thankful that Linda is willing to sacrifice her own needs for those of the family. But she is caught in a whirlwind of emotions. She lives in a world that is not of her making. Her family has not consciously decided to sacrifice her, but that is what they are doing. They have enough problems already—they do not want to hear anything from her that will make their mission more difficult.

As Linda tries in vain to balance her needs with those of the family, she is aware that she is changing. She is a teenager with the urge to try her wings on for size. Biologically, she is designed to become independent, to push away from the family and try on new behaviors. But what is she to do? At the very time that she yearns to be her own person, her parents need her more than ever. Part of her wants to scream and rebel against the family rules. But such a response would be emotional suicide. Her family has a silent agreement about acting out. The sticky glue of codependence binds her to the family and its unhealthy restrictions.

Slowly but surely, Linda learns the rules that Subby has talked about. If we could hear her talk years later, she might say this to us:

> I watched my parents trying to make the family work, but it was too much for them. They could not keep my older brother from opting out. They didn't have the energy to really listen to the rest of us. There wasn't enough time or attention to go around. They were tired and irritable a lot of the time. I think they regretted having so many kids, but they figured that out too late. I learned to keep my mouth shut. The other kids needed more attention than I did. I just wanted the family to be happy, so I helped

out in any way I could. I learned how to make my parents happy. I just didn't figure out until much later that I didn't get the love and attention I needed. No one ever helped me understand my own emotions. I was never encouraged to be the person God designed me to be. I see things so much more clearly now that I am out of the family and on my own. But I know I lost something.

Children Carrying the Pain

In their wonderful book, *Kids Who Carry Our Pain: Breaking the Cycle of Codependency for the Next Generation,* Drs. Robert Hemfelt and Paul Warren examine the seeds of codependence that are sown in dysfunctional families. They suggest that children, without intention, are set up to carry their parents' pain. This cycle can continue for generations if it is not broken.

Each generation is stacked upon another like a multilayered cake. Each layer impacts the next. The boundaries between generations are porous, with values and beliefs seeping through to the next tier.

Fortunately, these patterns can be broken. For example, I knew little about my paternal grandparents. But I knew that my grandfather struggled horribly with alcoholism and died an early death as a result of the disease. I knew that this tragedy impacted my father deeply. He was robbed of a father's love and friendship as a young man. He loathed the snakelike grasp that liquor had upon his father and vowed to never let it impact his life. He passed on that fear to his children.

Additionally, my father was abandoned by his father and was left, in part, to raise himself. He did not have the comfort of two loving parents to help him navigate the complexities of adolescence. As a result, my father has always made himself available to his five children and assisted us in coping with the challenges and rigors of adulthood. I have no doubt that his huge heart was developed in the crucible of pain and rejection. His courage and strength allowed him to break the cycle.

Attention Hunger

Drs. Hemfelt and Warren go on to say that in addition to carrying their parent's pain, children hunger for attention. Getting lost is unhealthy for them. Hemfelt and Warren suggest that attention hunger is more than just the need for undivided attention; it is also a need for identity. Without an identity, children grow up confused about who they are and where they fit in the world.

The authors identify the basic needs of children as *time, attention,* and *affection.* These three primary needs cannot be met by other children. They must be met by nurturing adults.

> Attention hunger underlies the other aspects of a child's growth and development. This hunger can be filled by a relationship or attachment to parents.[9]

Hemfelt and Warren note that a variety of abuses within the family can choke a child's need for attention and be extremely damaging to the child. They are convinced that passive sexual abuse is more common in families than we might like to believe. Such conduct includes inappropriate sexual comments and a failure to respect boundaries of privacy. The father who won't allow his daughter to shower in privacy is clearly committing a sexual violation.

Attention hunger can also develop in an atmosphere filled with physical abuse. In such families, discipline may take the form of harsh physical punishment for wrongdoing. Parents may firmly state, "It didn't hurt me to be hit by a switch, and it won't hurt you either." But children learn to recoil and withdraw in fear of their parents' anger.

Verbal abuse is also more common than we would like to admit—even in Christian homes, where we would like to think words are seasoned with grace. Parents call their children names when they fail to behave. Parents' screams can hurt children deeply. A little fear goes a long way in preventing children from developing into healthy adults who speak their minds.

Emotional Incest

Another horrifying prospect for children carrying the generational pain of their parents is identified by Hemfelt and Warren as *emotional incest*. Some time ago, a woman in the midst of a divorce told me that she had told her children about the struggles she was having with their father. As her venom spewed from her, she justified her actions by telling me that the children "have a right to know." I said that her children were too young to know how to deal with the emotions she was sharing with them. Yet she defended herself by insisting that the father's actions would certainly impact the children as much as they impacted her. In her mind, she was only trying to prepare them.

Many parents vent their frustrations to their children in a similar manner in the name of "open communication." But when parents reveal what is happening in their marital relationship, they invariably try to align the child with their point of view in opposition to the other parent. This is terribly damaging and confusing to the child.

Another form of emotional incest concerns parental injunctions. These are messages from the parents that tell children they must grow up to meet a particular standard. The children are being used by the parents to solve a problem in the parents' past. For example, the parent may not have done well in sports as a youth, and now the child is expected to make up for the parent's shortcomings. These types of messages are clearly inappropriate and often conveyed unconsciously.

Drs. Hemfelt and Warren cite several characteristics of the emotionally incestuous family:

- Nurturance is reversed, flowing from child to parent.
- Parents lack good personal identity or solid boundaries.
- Children provide some or all of the three S's:

  1. *Structure:* Authority roles are inappropriate. Control is either lacking or overused. Kids fill adult roles.

  2. *Stability:* Parents are emotionally unstable, so the child stabilizes the family.

  3. *Security:* The child must act as mediator between the family and the outside world or between the family members. The child seeks safety from sources outside the family.

The rule of thumb is easy to remember: *It is never the child's job to be there for the parent. It is the parent's job to be there for the child.*[10]

A Child's Needs

No individuals are perfect, so no families are perfect. But we can do a better job of raising our children than we have done. Creating an environment where a child will prosper takes a great deal of love and effort. Many people seem to think that children will be fine if they are given a modicum of affection and attention, but this may not be true. A child needs certain essentials in order to develop in a healthy manner. Let's review some of the basics that a child needs in order to become a healthy adult, free from the difficulties of codependency.

Time

Many busy parents leave their children to raise themselves. Most families are two-income households, and the children often become latchkey kids. They do not receive the time with their mother and with their father that they need to develop a healthy sense of self-esteem.

In my work with families, I notice that parents offer their children bits of time, but rarely are they devoted to the child's individual needs. Parents are so tired and preoccupied that the time they offer to their children is diluted. If children sense that their parents are tired, they may adjust their needs accordingly. They may act out in order to get the parents' attention—even negative attention. Or they may disappear, becoming "the lost child." They sense that the parent does not really have the time to devote to them. When this happens, they will look elsewhere for attention.

Parents who accept their responsibility to "be there" for the child are refreshing. They may be weary, but they summon the energy to allot valuable time to the child. They are emotionally present and able to enjoy watching the child flourish under their watchful eye.

Attention

Parents must give not only their undiluted time but also their undivided attention to their children. Watchful parents notice the subtle nuances in children's behaviors, moods, and thoughts, and then they express loving concern for those things that are important to the children.

Developmental psychologists teach us that parents can "mirror" their children's emotional lives to help children articulate what they are feeling. In this way, parents can help children navigate difficult encounters with their peers and move beyond painful moods. When we notice our child sitting quietly after learning that she was not invited to a friend's party, we might say, "Sally, it looks like you are feeling kind of sad about not getting invited to Lucy's birthday party. I'll bet that really hurts, especially after you had already thought about what to give her for a present." We are mirroring her feelings and helping her find words to express them.

Obviously, giving undistracted attention is a rigorous enterprise. It requires that parents set aside their own agenda to enter the child's world. This requires focus and intention. Nothing is as important or as effective as giving the child undivided attention.

Affection

We know that children are desperate for affection. When they don't receive affection from their parents, children will seek out destructive substitutes.

A healthy, loving touch doesn't cost. To see a child sit with a loving parent who offers touch generously is to see a child wrapped in an affirming presence.

Just as time is required to offer attention, time is necessary to offer affection. Hurried affection does little for the child.

Reflection

As you read this book, you may be stirred emotionally. Perhaps you remember situations when you did not receive the time, attention, and affection that you deserved and needed. By recognizing these places of hurt, you can allow the healing to begin. You can identify the destructive patterns that were set in motion long ago, and you can alter faulty beliefs. With an adult mind, you can make choices that are healthier for you and your entire family.

Begin by identifying the destructive beliefs you learned long ago. As you come to understand these beliefs, you will be prepared to replace them with healthier ones. You can learn to...

- talk openly about your thoughts
- share your feelings with someone who is safe
- trust others who will be there for you emotionally
- create a new, loving family with healthy rules

God has given us a model for healthy family functioning. He designed an order to the home in which children are protected, loved, and nurtured, free from the weight of codependent urges to protect others. However, this design is not always followed. Let's learn more about what happens when children are raised with codependent tendencies.

Chapter Two

The Pleasing Personality

*One crowded hour of glorious life
is worth an age without a name.*

THOMAS OSBERT MORDAUNT

Cindy sat alone at the kitchen counter, sipping a cup of coffee. The children and her husband were still asleep. She usually enjoyed these quiet, early morning hours, but today, the darkness that enveloped the house reflected her mood. She wondered how she was going to work up the courage to talk to her husband. How could she explain to John how discouraged she had become in recent months? And how could she reveal her fears without him becoming angry?

He had watched as she had gone to counseling, hoping that she would "get her act together." If anything, she felt more unraveled and discontented. She had hoped that counseling would provide a quick fix. She now saw her life more clearly, but the picture was not a pleasant one. She was more aware than ever of her unhappiness. And so she listened for his stirrings, waiting for a chance to talk with him about changes that might save their marriage. Her heart raced as she heard noises from their bedroom.

When John rolled over in bed, he noticed that Cindy was gone. He glanced at the clock. Seven in the morning. Time to get up and get ready for church. *I'm an usher today—better wear a shirt and tie.* He took a few minutes to wipe the sleep from his eyes before wandering out into the kitchen.

"What are you doing up so early?" he asked. "Did you have trouble sleeping?"

"Yes, I did."

"What's the matter?"

"Can we talk?" He nodded. "I don't know any other way to say this, but I'm not happy. I need to make some changes that I'm not sure you will like."

She watched as John grimaced. He put his left hand on his hip, something he always did when he was upset.

"You've spent a fortune on counseling, and you still aren't happy?"

As John's tone rose, she felt herself becoming tense. She reminded herself to stay with the process, to practice what she had learned in counseling, and to tell him what she wanted.

"I need to take better care of myself, John. I need to talk about how we manage our home and family. I need you to go to counseling with me to figure some things out. It's not all about you. It's about changing the way I've been for most of my life. It's about changing some bad habits we have in our relationship."

"This is a great way to start a Sunday," John said. He walked out of the kitchen and started getting ready for church.

The following day they arrived for their first counseling session. John's mood hadn't changed much from the previous morning.

"So, it's come down to this," John muttered as he sat down in my office. He immediately poured out his frustrations. After nearly 30 years of marriage, his wife had suddenly announced that she was tired of pleasing everyone else while she suffered inside. She said that things had to change because she couldn't take it any longer. His words were loaded with sarcasm.

He was shocked, hurt, and even a bit tearful. *What does this mean?* he wondered. *How long has she felt this way? What will change now?*

He turned and faced the window, stroking his graying beard. He became distant, caught up in his own bewilderment. He glanced back at his wife as she continued her saga of emancipation.

John probably knew that something was changing when Cindy started attending counseling without him some months ago. She began reading books on boundaries and assertiveness. She encouraged him to attend Sunday school classes on marriage enrichment. She even went away on a silent retreat to develop a deeper spirituality.

Much of it still seemed confusing to him. He saw little wrong with their relationship. He had thought his wife was happy enough. But her tone of voice told the real story.

I reviewed with him some of the history she had revealed to me during the earlier sessions of counseling.

"John," I said, "it seems that Cindy has been ignoring her own emotions and opinions for so long that she is slowly losing herself in the marriage. She is not here to blame you. It's not your fault. It's not anyone's fault. In fact, as I understand it, Cindy has struggled with a pleasing personality for many years. It probably started when she was a child. So you don't need to feel blamed or wrong. You two have simply developed some patterns that will take some work to undo. And you will both have to agree to work on creating some new, healthier patterns of relating."

Cindy tried to explain to John what had happened to her over the years. As a child, she had learned to be the caregiver. The only girl in a family with three brothers, she was expected to wait on the men. It was part of their culture. The women fixed the meals, cleaned the home, and generally cared for the family. Today, women in her family were expected to hold down a job as well. The result was a growing sense of exhaustion, resentment, and loss of her own identity.

"Losing yourself?" John questioned. "That doesn't make sense to me. You've been doing exactly what you have wanted to do. How can you lose yourself?"

John struggled to understand, and so do many people who suffer from pleasing personalities. One day, they wake up with an increasing sense that something is wrong, yet they are confused. How can they be dissatisfied when they are living the life they have chosen?

John and Cindy are typical of many couples. Many marriages consist of two income earners, though one of them, most often the woman, is also expected to care for the family and home. Driving kids to soccer practice and piano lessons, attending parent-teacher conferences, and working a full-time job are enough to wear down the hardiest person. This may be the life a woman has chosen or was encouraged to take, but now this existence is slowly choking the life out of her. Tired of pleasing others and feeling increasingly dissatisfied, she finally realizes she needs a change.

Traits of the Pleasing Personality

In chapter 1 we discussed some of the ways a person can be set up to please others and develop traits of codependency as a result. Most of us experience this to some extent, though we are usually unaware of what is happening. This book will help you identify those unhealthy personality traits that cause you to treat yourself in destructive ways. This is the essence of codependency, or the pleasing personality: *a pattern of pleasing others by setting aside your needs and well-being, to your detriment.*

As the weeks went by, I was able to make better sense of why Cindy had become so unhappy. She was discouraged and slightly depressed—a situation common to many women. And for similar reasons. Clearly, setting aside your desires temporarily in the service of others is not a problem. The Scriptures call on us to do so. But to do so to your own detriment, on an ongoing basis, leads to disaster. Think of Cindy as you look at this list of traits offered by Anne Wilson Schaef, author of *Co-Dependence: Misunderstood–Mistreated:*

- external referenting
- caretaking
- self-centeredness
- control issues
- denied feelings
- dishonesty
- being central
- gullibility
- loss of morality
- fear, rigidity, and judgmentalism[1]

External Referenting

Schaef is so concerned about *external referenting* that she believes most other traits of codependency fall under this one. *External referenting* means defining yourself by the way other people evaluate you. It means being completely preoccupied with what others think. If we don't have firm personal convictions about our own significance and worth, we will look to others to assure us that we are important to them.

Relationship Addiction

One example of external referenting is *relationship addiction.* Here we see the person who is willing to do *anything* to maintain a relationship, even if the relationship is debilitating to them. In relationship addiction we give away too much of ourselves. We are willing to do anything for the other person without regard for the long-term impact on our personality.

In my counseling practice, I commonly meet women who have had serial relationships with troubled men. Even though some men have no ability to truly love or give of themselves, women still love them. When these relationships falter, as they always do, the women wonder why. They do not understand two of the reasons that the relationships fail: The men are incapable of truly giving of themselves or building a healthy relationship, and the women have given too much of themselves to the relationship. These women have attempted to please others—at their own expense.

External referenting carries many other problems with it. Codependents do not know where they end and others begin. They have no clear boundaries to help them understand what is good for them and what is not, boundaries that establish what they are responsible for and what they are not. Consider this example:

Diane asked Angela to come over to her house for dinner, explaining that she needed to talk. Unfortunately, Diane asked Angela to come over in the evening, after work, when Angela was already exhausted. As Angela weighed the request in her mind, she realized that although her friend needed her, and she wanted to help, she also had a family that needed her care. She hadn't spent quality time with her husband for several days, and their children both needed help with school projects.

After struggling with her decision, Angela called Diane back and asked if they might meet a day later when she could make proper arrangements. Sometime later, Angela found out that Diane's feelings had been hurt that she did not drop everything to come to her assistance. Angela felt guilty. She wondered if staying home to take care of herself and her family had been the right choice.

This scenario is all too common. The tug of demands upon us is frequent and difficult to manage. It calls for us to be clear about who we are, to understand what is best for us and the ones we care about, and to make healthy choices. I believe that Angela made the right choice. I am not suggesting that we should be indifferent to our friends—quite the contrary—but we must weigh our resources carefully.

Taking on other people's problems can be very tempting. When we are close to people, we may have trouble letting them have their own feelings. The codependent wants to take away other people's pain. In some cases, codependents may literally feel another's pain. Codependents cannot feel at ease until they have helped others feel better. Surely this is taking compassion too far.

Impression Management

Another form of external referenting is what Schaef calls *impression management*. It means acting strictly with regard to what others will think of us. Insecure and plagued by flagging self-esteem, we look to others to validate our self-worth. Because we may distrust our own perceptions and feelings, we rely on others to determine how we behave or what we think.

The Scriptures remind us that we are infinitely valuable because God created us and is always with us (Psalm 139:1-18). He loves us and has given us a privileged place in creation (Psalm 8:3-5). Also, we are not to conform to other people's expectations but to be transformed from the inside out as God renews our minds (Romans 12:2).

Caretaking

Perhaps the hallmark of both the pleasing personality and codependency is the need to take care of other people. The problem is not our desire to help. Rather, when we take care of others, we sometimes forget to take care of ourselves as well. During my counseling sessions with Cindy, she told me how she exerted control in the midst of family difficulties. When the family needed a leader, Cindy stepped in as the caretaker to run the show. She even did this in her extended family. Her family members simultaneously loved and resented her for taking control.

The family needs and looks to the caretaker to manage things. Caretakers see a need and fill it. Caretakers don't seem to notice or don't care that their own well is dry—that they are parched and panting for water. They see a job to be done and they do it. Only later will they complain about having to do everything themselves.

What is wrong with this kind of behavior? Sometimes nothing, sometimes everything. When the caretaker gives because she feels valuable only when she is indispensable, her behavior is destructive. When she gives simply because she sees a need, but has not carefully considered whether she is truly able to help, this too will lead to problems. Conversely, when she feels a calling to help, when she has a special gift and gives from her abundance, this can be a wonderful thing for all concerned.

One of the best illustrations of caring versus caretaking is offered in the book of Luke where we read about Jesus' encounter with Mary and Martha. Here we read that Martha was busy caretaking and being "worried and upset about many things" (Luke 10: 41). To gain peace of mind, she spent all of her time taking care of things for people. The Lord shows his love for her by helping her set priorities, which, at that time, meant sitting at His feet with Mary and listening to Him. Everything else was just a distraction. Acting like a martyr in her caretaking would be of no value to herself or to Jesus.

Self-Centeredness

As the weeks of counseling went by, Cindy began to see that people with pleasing personalities attempt to keep everyone happy. They especially try to keep everyone happy *with them!* When their attempts fail, they feel guilty, angry, and hurt. When those around them are not doing well, they are not doing well. This burden is more than anyone can successfully carry.

Cindy walked through her codependent marriage on eggshells. She felt responsible for her husband's bad moods. She was especially tuned in to his anger. If he was upset about the house being messy, she felt guilty and fearful. If he thought the kids were too noisy, she tried to calm them down. If they didn't have enough money in their account, she wondered what she could do differently to magically balance the checkbook. She unconsciously believed that she had the power to make everything turn out right.

Of course, if you were to suggest that she was self-centered, she would vehemently deny it. In fact, the very thought would be repulsive to her. Of course she is not self-centered—she spends an inordinate amount of time caring for others! How could anyone make such an accusation? But think about it. She is preoccupied with others—with winning their approval. Pleasers pride themselves on being selfless—quite a self-centered perspective!

Control Issues

Yet another trait of the pleasing personality concerns the issue of control. As Schaef says, "Co-dependents are supreme controllers. They believe they can and should be able to control everything! As situations become progressively chaotic, co-dependents exert more and more control."[2]

Remember little Jessica from chapter 1? Even as a young girl, she believed that if she was good enough, she could lessen the tension in her parents' marriage. She wondered if her brothers' behavior was somehow her fault. Perhaps if she kept quiet and was nice, her family would have more peace

Of course, the family tension had nothing to do with Jessica. She had no power to make things better. Only her parents had the power to make things right.

Because people pleasers cannot control their worlds, they are prone to feel inadequate and depressed. They only look outward and spend too little time managing their own moods. They try to manage other people's moods—an impossible task.

One of the most powerful helps for those struggling with code-pendency is the Serenity Prayer. It is especially useful and powerful because it reminds us to focus on those things that we have control over and to let go of those things that we do not.

Serenity Prayer

God grant me the serenity
to accept the things I cannot change,
courage to change the things I can,
and wisdom to know the difference.
Living one day at a time,
enjoying one moment at a time,
accepting hardships as the pathway to peace.
Taking, as He did, this sinful world
as it is, not as I would have it,
trusting that He will make all things right
if I surrender to His Will,
that I may be reasonably happy in this life
and supremely happy with Him
forever in the next.
Amen.

REINHOLD NIEBUHR

Cindy wondered what life would be like now that she was trying to change old habits. She wondered what would happen to her marriage. If she stopped trying to please others, if she let go of trying to control things she could not control, her life would feel incredibly empty. She may be afraid to face these changes, and choose instead to continue her codependent behavior. On the other hand, she might fill up her life in a meaningful way by

- developing a stronger spiritual life
- establishing a strong sense of identity
- working on her love relationship
- discovering ways to create joy in her life
- finding fulfilling work
- building healthy friendships
- working on conflict resolution skills
- creating a healthy financial plan
- setting goals

Denied Feelings

During Cindy's initial weeks of counseling, her dammed-up emotions finally began to flow freely. Feelings long denied now seemed to take over her life. Because people pleasers look outward, and because they have worked long and hard taking care of others, they rarely give a lot of time or energy to nurturing their inner life. They spend little time considering what they feel or want. To many, the idea of listening to their feelings and tuning in to their own life sounds strange. "Nurture my inner life?" they ask. "What does that mean?"

It means taking time every day to reflect upon your life. It can be done by journaling, which many have found to be a useful daily practice. It can be done in prayer—a dialogue with God. It can be done by simply sitting quietly, perhaps with the Scriptures on your lap, considering how God may be moving in your life. What are your hopes and dreams? What are your anxieties and concerns? What is God telling you to do?

In my counseling practice, I meet many people who are living in a daze. They are not truly alert or alive. They live like robots, going through the motions, day in and day out. What is the effect of such living? Emotional and spiritual depression. Such lives often lack the joy that comes from being led by the Spirit of God and knowing the fruit of the Spirit.

A favorite author of mine, deceased priest and visionary Henri Nouwen, epitomized this sensitivity to his inner life and to the guidance of the Spirit. His writings are filled with vibrancy, reflecting a kinship with Christ that created a sense of abundance and immediacy. Listen to his words:

> Here we come to see what discipline in the spiritual life means. It means a gradual process of coming home to where we belong and listening there to the voice, which desires our attention...The great mystery of fecundity is that it becomes visible where we have given up our attempts to control life and take the risk to let life reveal its own inner movements. Whenever we trust and surrender ourselves to the God of love, fruits will grow. Fruits can only come forth from the ground of intimate love.[3]

Fecundity, or fruitfulness, requires that we let go of the strains and struggles of this world and listen to our inner spirit. This will give our lives new direction, peace, and joy.

Dishonesty

The last thing you would expect to see in a card-carrying codependent is dishonesty. I recently attended a family reunion where I introduced a dear friend to my extended family. Unfortunately, this led to a big misunderstanding about why I had brought this friend to the reunion. Rather than confront the gossip, which would have taken more courage and effort than I cared to muster, I glossed over much of the tension. I withdrew and told myself that I was fine and that I was protecting other people's feelings, but in reality I was harboring a grudge and pulling away from primary members of my family, giving them the cold shoulder. For a short time I acted codependently, but soon I realized that I needed to make a phone call to clear up my hurt feelings.

Melodie Beattie, in one of her books on codependency titled *Codependents' Guide to the Twelve Steps*, talks about other ways codependents are dishonest. She says, "So much of my codependency centered around feeling that I had to be perfect. When I feel this way, I make myself crazy. And I hide the imperfect side of myself from myself and others."[4] Talking to others is easy for Beattie when she feels good, but being vulnerable and asking for help is difficult for her when she feels weak. Like me, she needs to talk to others and show the side of herself that she would rather not show. That is honesty!

Being Central

Codependents need to be needed. That is part and parcel of this "dis-ease." Being in the limelight is quite addicting. A pleaser experiences a surge of power when she knows that other people look to her to manage things. She feels like the engineer on a train, the captain of an airliner, or the chief chef at a fancy restaurant. Everything revolves around her.

Being central, of course, has its costs. It means being "on" a lot, being available at other people's beck and call. Having others depend upon you for so many things can be exhausting. Many believe that is why codependents have a higher propensity to become ill. They are often weary from dealing with the excessive responsibilities on their plate.

Cindy reflected on her life and slowly came to realize how much energy she spent thinking about others. She felt run-down, tired from playing such a large role in her immediate and extended families.

She enjoyed some of the excitement of being where the action is, but she did not like the price she was paying.

Many pleasers have grown up with family members who refuse to accept responsibility. That is why pleasers have problems dealing with responsibility. They are not unwilling to take it on; rather, they are unable to let it go. Growing up with those who were not responsible, they learned to take up the slack and become overly responsible.

Gullibility

Schaef is the only author I know of who associates gullibility with codependence. If you are reading this book because you believe it may be describing you to some extent, considering yourself gullible may be difficult. *I can't be*, you may say. But consider the possibilities.

Pleasers can stay overly involved in spite of the overwhelming negative consequences because they expect a positive outcome. They are exhausted, people do not appreciate their efforts, their family life suffers—but none of these matter because everything will have a happy ending. Schaef says, "Co-dependents are notoriously bad judges of character, because they see what they want to see and hear what they want to hear."[5]

Counseling people with a pleasing personality is difficult because of their denial. They build elaborate belief systems to support their codependent behaviors. Until they come to the end of their rope, they can rarely see things as they really are.

I am reminded of a woman who was hopelessly enmeshed with her grown son. She and her husband were having severe marital problems because she insisted on bailing their son out at every turn. His drug addiction had led to serious financial and legal problems. No matter. She believed that a little more financial support from them would solve his problems. "I can't let him suffer out there," she would say. "You don't know what it's like for a mom to have a son who is hurting."

I could hardly argue with her. She justified her actions in spite of the marital conflict they caused and the destructive effect her enabling was having on her son. She was gullible enough to believe that he would place himself in treatment any day. He hasn't yet.

Loss of Morality

When we have an overwhelming need to please others, we are almost always dishonest. We lie about our motives. We lie about our intentions. Most importantly, we lie to ourselves about what is truly important.

In his bestseller *The Four Agreements,* Don Miguel Ruiz states that we must learn to be impeccable with our word. Any deviation from it is cause for alarm and a separation from our self. Lying is a form of dishonesty, and thus a loss of morality. He shares many examples of people who rely on others to tell them what to think and believe. By doing so, they lose touch with what is true and right.[6]

In a previous book of mine, *Men Just Don't Get It—But They Can: Nine Secrets Every Woman Should Know,* I wrote of the importance of being utterly truthful with yourself about your problems. The same truth applies here. Telling ourselves the truth is harder than we might imagine. To please others we must skirt the truth, embellish the good points, and minimize the harsh realities. But doing that means we lose part of ourselves in the process—we lose our morality.

Cindy finally admitted the time had come to be honest with John. She realized she was being dishonest by pretending to be happy and continuing to play the roles she had always played. She was not being true to her calling, to the core person she knew herself to be. She needed to speak the truth to her husband and family.

Fear, Rigidity, and Judgmentalism

The scene is the Galilean countryside, an arid, dusty landscape. The culture has been in place for generations. The religious beliefs are firmly established, and the people know how they are supposed to think and behave.

Into this parched land walks a man unlike any other. He looks straight into the eyes of the religious authorities and says, "You have heard it said...but I say..." He speaks truth that His hearers brand heresy, and this ultimately leads to His arrest and execution. This man was the Christ, and He still challenges us today to be careful of fear, of rigidity, and of judgmentalism.

> Do not judge, or you too will be judged. For in the same way you judge others, you will be judged, and with the measure you use, it will be measured to you. Why do you look at the speck of sawdust in your brother's eye and pay no attention to the plank in your own eye? How can you say to your brother, "Let me take the speck out of your eye" when all the time there is a plank in your own eye? (Matthew 7:1-4).

Codependents are notorious for rigid, judgmental attitudes that spring from fear. Because they are so fearful of losing their self-esteem, they cling to rigid beliefs in an attempt to control their world and yours. They try desperately to hold on to everything they have constructed. They believe that they are needed and in command.

Many of us have experienced the sticky grip of a friend who wants to tell us how to think. Imagine for a moment being utterly truthful with a friend about a problem in your life. As you tell your story, practice being completely honest. *Do not* tell the story as though you were the innocent victim, the wounded one. Tell it like it is. Admit that you have participated in the exchange of volleys that left you hurting. You know your malicious intent, your sharp words, and the venom that lurks in your heart.

Now imagine that same friend proceeding to scold and shame you. She tells you exactly what you must do, precisely what action to take, as if you had no other options. In doing so, she subtly belittles. In short, she judges you and lets you know that you are less than her. How do you feel? What do you think? You have been subjected to shame-based judgment—a deadly weapon in a codependent's hand. Recognizing the codependent's strategy allows you to begin to change this destructive process. Seeing it in yourself can open your eyes to the truth.

Reflection

Cindy and John are talking. The issues are difficult, but at least they are out in the open. The situation is scary for both of them as they tiptoe into a new relationship. Some days are discouraging; others provide a bit of hope. Both now see that change is essential. As they look back on their marriage, they recognize the traits of the codependent relationship. They can identify with what noted author and codependency expert Sharon Wegscheider-Cruse says in her book *Choicemaking*. According to Wegscheider-Cruse, the codependent leads a life with the following characteristics. Take a moment to reflect on your own life as you read this list.

- an inability to have spontaneous fun
- problems with intimacy
- an inability to know what is normal
- an exaggerated need for approval from others
- confusion about decision making
- black-and-white judgments
- fear and denial of anger

- lies and exaggeration
- fear of abandonment
- a tendency to look for people to take care of
- a need to control self and others[7]

This list overlaps much of what I have shared from the work of Anne Wilson Schaef. Clearly, people pleasers aren't as happy as they would be if they learned to live their own lives. That is precisely what this book is about. And it is possible for you.

The traits of codependency offered in this chapter may seem overwhelming, but I hope that you will allow the content to sink in and spur you on to growth. Unfortunately, to break through codependency, you must first break it down. Only when the old way quits working will you be ready to try a new approach. Are you ready for change? You may feel that the task is too great, but the truth is that you can conquer the problem, one step at a time.

Chapter Three

Getting Lost in Your Marriage and Family

The value of marriage is not that adults produce children but that children produce adults.

PETER DE VRIES

Panic filled her eyes. All she could see was a sea of legs in blue denim. She grabbed one for dear life, and for a moment she was content. She looked up, hoping to see the reassuring face of her mother. But she did not. Her big blue eyes widened, and she let loose a bloodcurdling scream that carried every ounce of her fear.

Being lost is incredibly frightening. As children we would do almost anything to keep from feeling lost, to avoid that terrifying, adrenaline-charged grasp for our mother's leg. As toddlers we ventured into the world, but most of us never strayed so far that we did not know exactly where our mother was. If she slipped out of view, even for a moment, we would start to panic and cry out.

Getting lost is no fun for adults either. We may be more secure and more willing to exercise a spirit of adventure—to take greater risks—but we usually stay within a ring of comfort. We still want to avoid feeling too far out on the edge. We repeatedly travel in many of the same circles so we don't have to face anything too new or risky. We can be surprised to discover that even though we walk the same well-worn paths, we may be losing our way. How could that happen? Life changes. Our needs change. We need to reflect upon where we are and what our daily needs are. Examine the following scenario and consider how your life may be similar.

Alice

Alice was 45 years old, a well-built woman of modest means who came to see me for counseling. Her nylon jacket appeared several years old and was heavily soiled on the sleeves. The bags under her eyes and the slump of her shoulders made her appear older than her age. She had never been in counseling before and wondered if it was right for her now. She told me that she had debated coming for many months. Her husband, Jake, had suffered a major industrial accident several years earlier. He had injured his back falling from some scaffolding, leaving him out of work and in chronic pain. Surgeries had alleviated some but not all of the pain. He would like to be active in his shop rebuilding things, but now he must watch his activity carefully.

This event had tragically altered Alice and Jake's financial and emotional lives. They struggled to make ends meet on the state industrial accident insurance program—a considerable challenge for a couple with three children in school. The entire family felt the effects of his accident.

As we discussed why she had sought counseling, I quickly saw that the accident was not the heart of the matter. The accident merely revealed issues that had lain dormant until the catastrophe brought them to the surface. Her husband had recovered from the accident, but their marriage wasn't the same.

Until this traumatic event, Alice and Jake had enjoyed a vibrant and rich sense of connection. She had doted on him and he expected many favors, but she felt that he appreciated her efforts and generally made her feel loved in return. However, after the accident, things began to change. Jake gradually became more preoccupied with his problems and less tuned in to the well-being of their marriage. He became short with her and more irritable. He planted himself in front of the computer or television and withdrew from the family.

As Alice told her story, she told me she now felt taken for granted. She had always been the caretaker in their marriage, but she had felt appreciated. Now Jake had become more self-centered and less concerned about how she was doing. She felt that instead of being a helpmate, she was just a maid. Jake expected her to prepare all the meals and depended on her to keep the house running. He lacked initiative and seemed somewhat depressed.

Alice shared how her role as a mother had changed as well. Their children, now teenagers, were very involved with their own lives. They expected her to taxi them from one sporting event or friend's house to another. By the time Alice came to see me she was seething.

Alice and I reviewed how she had become lost in the familiar terrain of family life. It had not happened all at once (it rarely does). She explained that she had grown up in a traditional family where women were expected to wait on the men. Women busied themselves with cooking, cleaning, and caretaking. They followed the culturally prescribed way of life. If they were not busy, they often felt guilty that they might be neglecting something or somebody.

As we explored Alice's family history, she realized that she had consistently ignored her needs for the sake of her family. She made certain that others were having fun before she relaxed, allowed others to make important decisions, went along with what others wanted to do, and hid her anger and frustration. She had never really thought of living differently—until now.

During her counseling sessions, Alice began to see that this problem had taken years to develop. The storm had been brewing since childhood, and the accident simply brought things to a head. Let's listen to Alice tell her story.

I have been caring for my husband and children for years. I always wanted to please them. It gave me great satisfaction to set a wonderful table and have the family together. I went the extra mile to see the kids happy. I wanted Jake to be able to come home from work and put his feet up and relax. If he was relaxed, the whole family was relaxed. I never realized I might resent having to care for everyone else, but I do. I look back and see that no one has taken care of me. I didn't even take care of myself. I ignored my own opinions and feelings when I was growing up, and I've done the same thing as an adult. I'm finally beginning to understand that this is not the way I want to live.

I asked Alice if she had asked anyone to pay attention to her needs. Had she ever asked for help?

Never. I assumed that if I did things for others, they would do things for me. Maybe I thought that helping everyone else was its own reward. I assumed that the family would think like I do—that they would take care of others and do what needs to be done. It's taken me all this time to realize that I was the only one who was thinking this way. My husband and children have no problem asking for help, but they don't offer much of it. And now I see that I created this situation.

Symptoms of Getting Lost

Alice is lost. She came to my office with deep feelings of dread and anxiety, as if she were desperately searching for her mother's soothing face. She was trying to navigate the unfamiliar terrain of other people's needs and wishes without the landmarks of her own emotions and opinions. She needed help finding her way back home.

In the last chapter, we saw many reasons we can lose our way, many of them linked to the codependent or pleasing personality. Perhaps you were able to relate to a few of them and develop a plan for changing. Let's look closely at the symptoms we suffer when we become lost in our marriage and family. These traits are cited in the book *Choicemaking* by Sharon Wegscheider-Cruse.

Inability to Know What Is Normal

Many women who come to see me have lost their way. They are often desperately looking for someone who can assist them in finding their way back home. Unfortunately, that is not always possible. Sometimes such dramatic changes have occurred that going back is not realistic. Sometimes a new path and a new home must be located.

Many women lose their sense of perspective. They can sense that things are not right, but they tell themselves that this is the way everyone lives. They are unsure of what they feel, unsure whether they are accurately analyzing the situation. They may also question whether they even have the right to be dissatisfied.

When we go hiking in the wilderness, veering a few degrees from the correct heading can cause us to become completely lost. Similarly, losing one's way in a marriage and family may occur subtly. Women rarely recognize how lost they are. They commonly say, "I have been living like this for years. I don't know any different. My husband tells me that things are fine, that we are a typical couple, and that I expect life to be a fairy tale. But I start to panic—is this really the best way to live?"

When Alice began to sense that things were wrong, she had to overcome her denial of the problem. In fact, she waited four years to begin counseling because she kept telling herself that things were not that bad. She used daily doses of denial to dull the ache of living a discouraging life. To make life tolerable, she decided her problems were normal. By the time she came to see me, she couldn't tell what was normal and right and what was not.

Like many others, Alice initially looked to me to tell her that she was not imagining the problem. "Am I crazy? Is this the way other women live? Should I be satisfied with things as they are?"

While I am willing to reassure these women that life is often intensely frustrating, I want them to acknowledge their own sense of right and wrong. I want them to trust their ability to judge the situation. I am aware, however, that many women have long distrusted their own opinion and have looked to other authorities to tell them how they should feel. But God has given each of us the ability to look at a situation and judge its merits. Our perception may have become skewed, but we can regain our focus. You can learn to trust your impressions again.

Mary Field Belenky, et al., in their book, *Women's Ways of Knowing*, note that women have been trained to "devote themselves to the care and empowerment of others while remaining 'selfless.' They have been taught, culturally, to silence their voice and wait upon others in the family and society."[1]

An Exaggerated Need for Approval

Being lost in a montage of differing opinions can be intimidating. Disagreeing with others can be difficult under the best of circumstances. In fact, many of us have been taught not to disagree with others—especially with authority figures. Because of previous learning and a shaky self-esteem, our need for approval often becomes exaggerated. As a result, a vicious cycle becomes established in many relationships.

A woman desires to please her husband because she enjoys the feelings that come from seeing his pleasure with her. Assume that she has an exaggerated need for this approval and that he likes to be in control. The cycle will happen again and again, and the pattern will become self-reinforcing: When she defers to him, he is pleased with this control and shows that he is happy with her. Both feel good. In fact, they believe they have found the key to a healthy relationship. Repeat this pattern thousands of times, and it becomes second nature.

Why do some people have an exaggerated need for approval? This can occur for any number of reasons, but the most common is a lack of self-esteem. For many, the risk of incurring someone's displeasure or wrath is simply too frightening. To preserve their self-esteem, they defer to others.

But what is wrong with deferring to others? Isn't that what we are called to do as Christians? This is only partially true. It is true enough to create a great deal of confusion. Let's be clear about our definitions.

Healthy Self-Esteem

Healthy self-esteem is not the same thing as an exaggerated sense of self-importance. Scripture challenges us repeatedly not to think too highly of ourselves. Rather, we are told to view ourselves "with sober judgment, in accordance with the measure of faith God has given to you" (Romans 12:3). Self-esteem, for our purposes, means having a clear sense about who we are. It means knowing the truth about our value as God's creation. Scripture repeatedly illustrates our value by calling us "children of God" and "royal priests" and by explaining that we are created in God's image. This is ample evidence of our innate worth. However, if our sense of self-esteem is predicated upon other people's opinions of us or our performance, we are doomed to feelings of failure.

We are called to "submit to one another out of reverence for Christ" (Ephesians 5:21), but this does not mean that we are to mistreat ourselves in the process. Just as we are called to use our gifts to serve the body of Christ, we are also challenged to care for ourselves (1 Corinthians 3:16-17; 6:19-20). We are the temple of the Holy Spirit and must meticulously care for our own well-being.

Finally, we must understand that unless we care for ourselves, we will not be able to adequately care for others. Scripture tells us this (Acts 20:28; 1 Timothy 4:16), and we also know it intuitively. Who can reach out to minister to others when they have not nurtured themselves with appropriate rest, sustenance, exercise, and social interaction? Although Jesus was capable of working miracles, we see His example of pulling away from the crowds so that He could rest and prepare for the rigors of His ministry.

We must treat ourselves and others as having special value. Anything less is intolerable. This is a biblical doctrine and essential for us to embrace as Christians.

Avoiding Decisions

"I don't know what I think anymore," many women tell me. "I used to be so decisive. I knew what I thought and was able to express it clearly. Not anymore. I worry about myself."

Another symptom of codependency and people-pleasing behavior is the avoidance of decision making. The ability to analyze a situation and determine a course of action is one of God's greatest gifts to us. However, a vicious cycle can easily develop in which one avoids making decisions. And the more you avoid making decisions, the harder breaking the cycle becomes.

My mother comes from a long line of wonderful caregivers. She has always been a servant, and she delights in meeting the needs of those who enter her home. If you walk away hungry from one of her Swedish buffets, something is dreadfully wrong. However, in recent years I have taken to teasing her about her indecisiveness. When the clan decides where we will have our next family outing, her reply is invariably "I don't care." I assume that to be true for her; she would prefer that others made the choice. But I want to know what she thinks. She is important to me, and I want her voice to be heard. So, when she asserts that she doesn't care, I give her a look that I am now able to get away with. "Come on, Mom," I say. "Tell us what you want." She will now smile and offer her opinion, but she remains hesitant to do so.

You may relate to my mother. You may have followed a pattern until you became lost and impotent in the decision matrix of the family. You may have said to yourself,

- It's not that important.
- I don't care.
- I can't decide.
- I want to make others happy.
- I don't know what I think.

But stop for a moment to consider a new path:

- The family needs to know what you think.
- Your opinion is worthwhile.
- When you flex your decision-making muscles, they become stronger.
- Your indecisiveness can be annoying to others.
- Making decisions is a way to express your personality.

Fear and Denial of Anger

Alice's anger was palpable in the room. When she spoke about her husband, Jake, she gritted her teeth. She chewed her fingernails to the quick. She had not slept soundly in months. Yet when I asked her if she were angry, she quickly replied, "Oh, no!" Codependents commonly deny their feelings. It seems to come with the territory.

Kay Marie Porterfield, in her book *Coping with Codependency*, says, "When we are codependent, we're so busy trying to escape our anger, shame, and pain that we have trouble knowing how we feel. On the surface we're numb, but deeper inside our feelings are eating away at us."[2]

I felt genuinely concerned for Alice. I could see her struggling with her feelings. Although she denied feeling angry, I could see the rage eating away at her. She consumed her rage as surely as her rage consumed her. Her feelings leaked out in her symptoms: the sarcastic way she talked about her husband, her excessive eating and lack of sleep, the way she scolded the children when she was unhappy. Yet she also felt a need to project an image of propriety toward him. How alone she must have felt as she held this torrent of trapped feelings inside.

Many women learned early in life to numb their feelings in order to cope. This numbness is a poor substitute for genuine hope in the face of ongoing adversity. Still, when the challenge of maintaining hope becomes overwhelming, many people simply opt to silence their own voice and retreat into numbness. And the longer a voice is numbed, the harder it is to regain.

Fear of Abandonment

The ultimate risk for the people pleaser is that others may disapprove of your thoughts and actions. They may look at you with a scrunched-up nose, furrowed brow, and icy stare to say, "You think what?" Or they may literally say, "You've got to be kidding!" I hope that you live in a world that will be accepting of your newfound efforts to be decisive. However, if that is not the case, voicing your point of view may mean risking emotional abandonment. It may mean risking the disapproval of some very important people in your life. This is a consequence you will have to consider if your happiness hangs in the balance.

Porterfield explains that codependents are people who need people. They have come to rely upon the complete acceptance of other people even though this extracts a high price. She says, "To make others like us, we become people pleasers. We would rather be the givers than the takers, whether of compliments, offers of help, or presents. We measure our worth by the people around us: If they approve of us, we must be okay; if not, something must be wrong with us."[3]

The fear of abandonment is not a trivial matter. We have been created to connect with others, and to risk rejection is a big deal. This is especially true when a relationship is critical to one's sense of well-being. Let's listen again to a recent counseling session with Alice as she struggled with asserting herself in her long-standing marriage.

"Your husband has become more irritable lately and now is rejecting you?" I asked.

"Yes," she said. "Things have gotten worse over the past four years, ever since the accident. I don't want to push him because he gets angrier when I ask him questions about our relationship. He says he doesn't want to talk about it. He shrugs his shoulders and says it's not important."

"So you feel you have to tiptoe around him?"

Alice grimaced and looked away. She clutched the covering of the armrest on her chair.

"I try to occupy myself with the kids and their activities, but I miss the closeness we had. I miss the walks we used to go on, the snuggling on the couch watching a movie. I feel like I've lost him. He doesn't talk to me much and seems to be withdrawing more and more. I know the accident is bothering him, but he doesn't want to talk about his feelings. I guess he has never been very good at talking about things that bother him. But now it's worse."

"What happens when you do talk with him?"

"I really don't talk with him much about us. He gets upset, and I can't stand to have him angry with me. He withdraws even more when he's unhappy."

"And you feel powerless. You can't talk to him about your problems, and you can't seem to stop him from withdrawing from you."

"I've been so upset lately that I asked him to come to counseling. He told me that he wasn't interested. He said that he had no intention of talking about our problems with a stranger and that I was making too much out of things. I'm afraid that if I make any demands on him he'll tell me to leave. I don't want to threaten 25 years of marriage. I don't want to be responsible for the kids losing their father. So I just put up with things the way they are. I don't see where I have much choice."

"Do you think he will change on his own, Alice?"

"I know that I am kidding myself. I guess I'm just not sure what to do."

Alice is facing a very difficult situation. Her husband is having his own crisis, and in the process he is creating another crisis for their marriage. Yet we shouldn't see his accident and subsequent dissatisfaction as being the primary cause of their problems. The accident simply crystallized his latent controlling and distancing nature. Jake and Alice were probably already heading for a crisis. Some event was bound to occur that would make Alice realize she was losing herself in the marriage.

We can also see that having three children storm into adolescence has compounded her problems. Their self-absorption leaves Alice feeling even more as if she is taken for granted. Undoubtedly, she and her husband have set the stage for the children to expect to be coddled—we need only look at her relationship with Jake to find proof of that—and this has left Alice feeling even more victimized. While the challenge is great, Alice must transform this crisis into a cry for change.

Need for Excessive Control

In our last chapter, we saw that control issues are central to codependence and the pleasing personality. This may seem utterly contradictory. How can we suggest that the codependent is seeking control when in so many ways he or she feels like they have lost control? But most codependents are working overtime to make things turn out just the way they want them to. They have a particular outcome in mind and are not happy when things go awry. They take these situations personally because they have an extraordinary investment in the outcome.

The codependent's well-being is dependent on others and, more importantly, on others doing well. By their behavior, codependents are saying, "When you're okay, I'm okay. When you're not okay, I'm not okay." To make sure they feel okay, they plan outcomes. They have a difficult time being flexible. In her bestseller *Women Who Love Too Much*, Robin Norwood sheds light on the interesting issue of control:

> When efforts to help are practiced by people who come from unhappy backgrounds, or who are in stressful relationships in the present, the need to control must always be suspected. When we do for another what he can do for himself, when we plan another's future or daily activities, when we prompt, advise, remind, warn, or cajole another person who is not a young child, when we cannot bear for him to face the consequences of his actions so we either try to change his actions or avert their consequences—this is controlling. Our hope is that if we can control him, then we can control our

own feelings where our life touches his. And of course.
the harder we try to control him, the less we are able
to.[4]

We can easily see why women are particularly prone to codependency. Perhaps they are inclined to this method of control because
so many men unconsciously seek to be mothered. Conversely, many
women need to play the mother's role. Fortunately, at any age, you
can learn to stop serving as a mother to overgrown children. This
is a necessary step in taking control of your life.

Women are not the only ones prone to codependency control
issues. I am reminded of a young man named Gene who came to
my office because he wanted his family to "get along better." He was
weary of the nonstop bickering among his four children. He desperately wanted harmony in the home. Initially, I thought his goal
was honorable. His wife thought the goal equally worthwhile, but
she was a bit more practical. "Kids will be kids, Gene," she would
say. "Let them be children while they are young enough to enjoy it."

Gene's desire for counseling was unusual for many reasons. First,
men do not generally come to me for help, although I was delighted
that he did. Second, they do not often come seeking greater unity
in their families. Again, I was glad that he was concerned enough
about the well-being of his family that he was willing to break this
stereotype.

Soon after he brought the family in for counseling, I realized
that his goals could not be realized. He obviously wanted his children to "like each other and get along." This was a wonderful ideal
but not terribly realistic. His children realized more quickly than
he did that his goals could not be accomplished. Almost immediately during the family session they announced that they could not
be forced to always like one another. They said that they loved each
other, but they were insightful enough to realize that they would
not always get along.

While Gene had one set of goals in mind when he came to counseling, he soon came to see that he had to work on something else entirely. He could not dictate how his children felt about one another. He discovered that he could manage their behavior, but he needed to loosen his expectations about their feelings. He also needed to let go of his desire to compel his wife to dictate the children's feelings. In short, he needed to let go of some control.

Problems with Intimacy

Codependents are terrified of being hurt, so they often have trouble with intimacy. This too may seem like a contradiction. People pleasers want to be accepted, they hate conflict, and they want others to like them. This would appear to be the perfect recipe for intimacy. But they often have trouble maintaining close relationships. This can be a bit complicated to understand.

Consider the delicate nature of a healthy marriage. Here we see a couple free to disagree with one another. They are permitted to function as separate and unique individuals.

God said that it was not good for man to be alone, so He created a helper suitable for him. God did not create another man to comfort Adam. Perhaps wanting to add some zest to Adam's life, God created a woman. Someone very different from him. The two separate and unique creatures were meant to complement one another.

Now consider what happens if one or both partners are unable to function as distinct individuals. What happens if one is preoccupied with harmony? What happens if one needs to please the other, instead of voicing opinions and offering gifts freely in the relationship? Furthermore, what will happen if one sends out the dual message, "Come close but stay away," as is often the case with codependents? The desire for intimacy hides under a fear of losing aspects of the personality that were so painfully won. This push-pull struggle creates enormous chaos in the marriage.

Many traits that accompany codependency can wreak havoc on a marriage. For example, avoiding conflict can be devastating to a relationship. Conflict must occasionally come out into the open to change destructive patterns that develop, as is the case with Alice and Jake. Every relationship is dependent upon the open display of emotion to create intimacy. When one or both partners avoid sharing emotions, genuine closeness is impossible.

Melody Beattie, in *Codependents' Guide to the Twelve Steps*, shares another interactive pattern that can impair relationships. "We may anticipate rejection when it is not forthcoming. We may fall into the trap of our old beliefs: that we are unlovable, incompetent, and undeserving. Those old beliefs are wrongs against ourselves, and they can do harm in our relationships."[5]

True intimacy, as designed by God, consists of two individuals coming together in vulnerability and transparency. Both people have a healthy sense of value because they know that they are esteemed by God and by their spouse. Love thrives in this safe and secure setting. You can experience true intimacy if you are willing to relinquish your people-pleasing behavior.

Controlling Men

Some relationships are particularly troubled by a pattern of behavior that deserves special attention. Dominating men control too many households. In these homes, women must shrink back to preserve their faltering sense of esteem.

Patricia Evans, noted author of *Controlling People*, helps us understand the dynamics involved in relationships where men are excessively controlling. She sets the stage by informing us, "When the truth of our being is clearly reflected to us, we know ourselves and trust ourselves. Our self-knowledge is enhanced and we remain connected to ourselves. We then have the ability...to resist controlling behavior."[6] However, if you have grown up needing the approval and affirmation of others in order to define yourself, you may be drawn to controlling people. And many men are ready and willing to control women.

Evans notes that controlling men tend to define the personalities of the women they control. The women willingly agree to remain lost. Instead of maintaining their own opinions, they allow the controlling person to tell them how to behave, think, and even feel. When the woman dares to assert her opinion, the man convinces her that she shouldn't have such "aggressive" thoughts. He criticizes her thoughts, her actions, and even her feelings. She can do little to please a controlling man because her independence violates his need to control.

Over time, controlled women learn to distrust themselves. They numb their feelings and act robotically. "Having learned to deny their own wisdom and having taken in other people's definition of them, without even realizing it, those who are disconnected from themselves construct an identity not grounded in experience but constructed out of, or in reaction to, other people's ideas, expectations, and values."[7]

Ceasing to exist spiritually and emotionally is tragic. It is the antithesis of what the Lord wants for us. It violates the precepts of the gospel and the sanctity of each and every life. If you find yourself in a stifling, controlling relationship, you can begin taking action by speaking up and sharing your thoughts, intentions, and feelings.

Why Are Men Controlling?

Upon first reading of this material, you may think a controlling man is diabolical. But this is rarely the case. Although the reasons why men are controlling are not easily explained, Evans suggests that

- Domineering men have a need to be right because they do not know themselves from within and are threatened by differing points of view. If we are able to remain connected to ourselves and to God, we are able to be wrong about some things without being overly threatened.

- Domineering men have a need to be one up because in order to feel superior they must not be challenged. Their self-esteem is so fragile that it cannot handle being questioned.

- Domineering men need to win because they need to be right. Winning is more than a game to controllers.

Controlling men employ a variety of tactics to maintain their power. Easily threatened, they may resort to different behaviors to avoid feeling vulnerable. As you begin to assert yourself and find your way, you may notice an escalation in a controlling man's tactics.

- Isolation—your friendships or outside activities may threaten him. He may demand that you come straight home from work, and he may be very disapproving of your friendships.

- Verbal abuse—he may use anger in combination with other tactics to frighten you. He may resort to name-calling or threats to make you feel vulnerable.

- Judgment—he may be overly critical of your actions. Nothing you do will warrant his acceptance or affirmation.

- Withdrawal—he may let you know that what you are doing is wrong. You will pay for it by his withdrawal.

- Spiritual abuse—he may use Scripture to manipulate you into complying with his wishes.

Let's revisit our discussion of Alice and Jake. Jake's self-esteem, his value of himself as a breadwinner, has certainly taken a beating as a result of his accident. This is partially responsible for his behavior toward Alice. However, his accident only brought out his controlling personality. His vulnerability resulted in a feeling of impotence, and he responded by punishing Alice. He blamed her for everything that went wrong in the home. He criticized her mercilessly. At other times he withdrew from her, indicating his displeasure in a passive-aggressive manner.

In my work with Alice, I emphasize that seeing herself as a victim will do no good, though to some degree she is surely being victimized. As she begins to find her way, she will need to believe that having feelings is okay, and she will need to identify the feelings she has kept hidden for so long. Her task is to use every situation as an opportunity to learn more about herself, relying on the Lord to give her insight and strength to assert herself and take appropriate action. When Jake's controlling behavior no longer works, he will no longer use it.

Setting Healthy Boundaries

In their groundbreaking book *Boundaries*, John Townsend and Henry Cloud instructed millions about the importance of setting boundaries.[8] This book struck a chord with readers who recognized the importance of being separate yet interdependent people.

The authors remind us that Scripture is replete with examples of boundaries, that God established this universe based upon boundaries. Geographical boundaries help us define where our property begins and ends. Emotional, spiritual, and physical boundaries help us determine what is and what is not our responsibility. Boundaries are wonderful ways to let people know who we are and who we are not.

If being controlled by others is a way to become lost, setting boundaries about who will exercise control over your life is a way to help you find yourself again. Declaring to others what is important to you, what you will tolerate, and what you will not is another way of setting boundaries.

Practice saying yes to things that are important to you and no to things that need to be eliminated from your life. This is an excellent way of reestablishing your identity in your relationship.

Reflection

You can begin the process of finding your way today. Begin by taking small, daily steps. Practice by making a list of...

- one or two things that you will say yes to because they are important to you
- one or two things that you will say no to because they need to be eliminated from your life
- three things that you appreciate about your partner, and one thing that you would like to see change

Chapter Four

Creating a Healthy Marriage

You are unique, and if that is not fulfilled,
then something has been lost.

MARTHA GRAHAM

I watched as the young couple walked hand in hand on the boardwalk along the waterfront park, laughing and exchanging whispers. Seagulls soared overhead, and on the water the fluttering sails of dozens of boats seemed to wave in honor of this couple's love. They were obviously lost in each other. No one else existed. Their affection defined their world.

Embryonic love is a passionate thing, filled with the wonderful rush of biochemicals. It is a time of youthful vigor and desire that are capable of creating an addictive wave of emotion. But that wave of emotion carries the possibility of deception. As the lovers gazed into each other's eyes, what were they seeing? Did they see each other's true self or merely some distorted reflection of what they wanted to see, perhaps even some idealized aspect of themselves?

The timeless sentiment of romantic love has been captured in many love letters. This one is from Sophia Peabody to the author Nathaniel Hawthorne, dated December 31, 1839.

What a year has this been to us! My definition of Beauty is, that it is love, and therefore includes both truth and good. But those only who love as we do can feel the significance and force of this.

My ideas will not flow in these crooked strokes. God be with you. I am well, and have walked far in Danvers this cold morning. I am full of the glory of the day. God bless you this night of the old year. It has proved the year of our nativity. Has not the old earth passed away from us?—are not all things new? Your Sophie.[1]

Can you feel the overwhelming passion? The exclusivity of romantic love? I do not wish to overanalyze or trivialize this joyful coupling. Romantic love is something wondrous and must not be hurried or cast off as immaturity. This symbiotic state is natural, expected, and helpful. It is the time when the glue is placed and set, binding the lovers' hearts to each other and setting the stage for advances in the relationship. If this early adoration did not exist, moving toward a committed marriage would be difficult.

Who has not felt moved when seeing lovers peer into each other's eyes and hearts? As observers, we may be caught off guard. We look and then turn away in embarrassment. At times, we are filled with emotion as well. Sometimes we feel disgust, wishing they would take their gushy affections someplace out of public view. Sometimes we feel jealous, wishing we had a small dose of their passion to infuse into our relationship. Sometimes we just shake our heads as we wonder at the childlike innocence of young love.

Indeed, young love is similar to a child's symbiotic relationship with his or her mother. The infant, for all intents and purposes, is indistinguishable from the mother and knows nothing, save their intimacy and his or her utter dependence upon the parent. A child's entire world and very existence is dependent upon the caring nurturance of the mother. Narcissism is expected. The world revolves around the infant, and, for the most part, both parent and child are content with that arrangement. Watch the new mother with her child and see the simple bliss there. The mother adores her infant child; the child is lost in the mother's embracing love.

Narcissus was a Greek demigod so beautiful that everyone fell in love with him, including himself. As the story goes, he fell in love with his own image in a pool of water and, transfixed, fell into the water and drowned.

All of us know people who are narcissistic. They parade around like proud peacocks, hoping that others will find them utterly beautiful. These people have invested an inordinate amount of energy in themselves—so much so that they cannot give their attention to another because they are in love with themselves. No relationship can survive when "It's all about me."

So when we see the young couple on the boardwalk listening intently to the other, watching for the slightest change in facial gestures and proclaiming their affirmations with smiles and embraces, we must encourage them. "Hold on to one another," we must say. "Embrace each other now, and learn all you can. Build your love and store it up. A time will come when you will begin to pull away into your separate worlds, and you must remember what you are feeling at this moment if you are to close the distance between you. It happens subtly, so beware."

Love at First Sight

Sometimes love blossoms from the outset. It seems to happen in an instant. The chemistry is undeniable, a connection that is healthy and right. In such cases, the relationship progresses to a mutual respect for each other's individuality.

But at other times, something else happens. Researchers call it "love addiction." Perhaps you know people who fall in love as often as they change their seasonal wardrobe.

What I am describing here is obviously not mature love. It is a compelling need to connect to another person. It is really a desire to lose ourselves in the arms of another, indefinitely. Susan Peabody, in her book *Addiction to Love*, says, "Because of this inner compulsion love addicts are impatient to bond with someone before they really get a chance to know him or her. I call this phenomenon 'love at first sight' or premature bonding."[2] Here we see another form of codependency, based on an unhealthy desire to merge—another tendency to please another that is hurtful to ourselves.

Peabody notes that this immature form of love usually overwhelms the people that addicts fall in love with, pushing them away or creating trauma if they realize that they have fallen in love with the wrong person and must end the relationship. She adds that these relationships often include a high level of drama and excitement. Love addicts are not really looking for love; they are looking for the rush that comes from being in love. They want the high that comes during the initial stages of a relationship. When the high is over, they go looking for another relationship to recreate the drama.

Kay Marie Porterfield, in her book *Coping with Codependency*, calls this phenomenon being instantly intimate. She adds:

> Sometimes codependents crave closeness so much that we overwhelm people, crashing through their boundaries like tanks smashing through fences in old war movies. We spend every minute we can with them, and when we can't be with them, we call. Ignoring their privacy boundaries, we quiz them about the details of their lives. We share our problems with them whether they want to listen or not. Demanding fierce loyalty, we can be jealous to the point of insisting that our new friends give up their other friendships, their hobbies, and their schoolwork.[3]

Obviously, codependency and love addiction are not what we are looking for when we search for a healthy relationship.

An Uneasy Dependence

Elise was a young woman of 25 who came to see me for symptoms of depression. She had been sleeping poorly, and her ability to concentrate was faltering. Her appetite had decreased, and she had lost ten pounds off an already slender body. I asked her about symptoms associated with anorexia and bulimia. She denied having an eating disorder, but I still had my suspicions. I noted that we might need to consider medications to remedy her sleep and appetite problems. She dismissed the idea and said that she would be fine.

I asked Elise to share more about what had brought her to counseling, and what might be causing her sleeplessness and loss of appetite. She shared the following story.

> I've been married for five years to a wonderful man. Michael is an account representative for a cell phone company. He works long hours, and they push him pretty hard to increase his sales. It seems like every year he works harder and harder, trying to be the best salesman the company has ever had. He's making more money but working more hours. We have two young children, and we hardly see him. Actually, we see him, but when we do he is thinking about work, or he's tired because of work, or he is sleeping so that he can get ready to go back to work. It seems like the kids and I get the leftovers of his life.

I listened as Elise shared her history with Michael. They had met at the company where he now worked; she too had worked there for a number of years. They enjoyed a long and happy courtship and then got married. Soon after, Elise quit work to be at home full-time with their young children.

"It sounds like you both have always been busy," I said.

"Yes, but the current situation is ridiculous. We used to find time for each other. That's not the case anymore."

"You're upset that he doesn't give quality time to the children?" I asked.

She paused. "Well, that and the fact that he doesn't seem to put me first in his life. When we were dating, he would sacrifice anything for me. He used to buy me gifts, surprise me with things he knew I enjoyed, and he made me feel special. Now, he seems to take me for granted."

"Marriage can feel like that at times," I said. "Couples get into doing their own thing and forget that they need to continue creating warmth and affection in their relationship, or it can stagnate. Have you talked to Michael about your feelings?"

"Yes, and he feels badly about it. He wants to spend more time with me, but the company has quotas, and Michael is never satisfied unless he meets or beats them. He is very goal oriented and wants to provide a great living for us."

"Is he willing to work on the relationship with you?"

"Yes, he says he is willing. But I feel lost without him. Now that I'm not working it seems harder. I've lost touch with most of my friends from work because I don't get a chance to see them anymore."

"So you're feeling lonely, and you don't have any close friends to confide in. And you spend most of your time changing dirty diapers and preparing meals. It sounds like your life pretty much revolves around your family. What do you do for yourself?"

"Not much." Elise glanced at a painting I had on the wall. She sat silent for a few moments. "I guess I came to rely on Michael for my social life. He became my best and, really, my only friend. Probably not the best situation."

"It is an easy thing to have happen," I told her. "It's natural to look to your spouse to be your best friend. That's the way it should be. But we need others in our lives to give us support too. We have to maintain some friendships apart from the one with our spouse."

Breaking the Addiction

We spent the next few sessions exploring Elise's uneasy dependence on her husband. We examined her history of losing herself to love and, subsequently, giving up her identity to the relationship.

She had been the oldest of three children, and when her parents divorced, she became the caretaker for the family because her mother worked full-time. Now she had slipped into being the caretaker for the family again, giving up the activities and friendships that had been important to her.

We invited her husband to join us in counseling. Michael was more than willing to participate and readily admitted that he had placed too much importance on his job. Although he was not overly excited about scaling back, he knew that his family missed him. Elise and the kids were important to him, and he was willing to make changes.

However, Michael being home more often didn't solve the problem. After he cut back on work and spent more hours with his family, Elise still found herself relying on him as her sole source of friendship and support. We discussed this at several sessions, and she realized that she needed to redevelop some of her old friendships, perhaps take an evening class at the local college, and then enjoy quality time with her husband. Elise found that she had a propensity to lose herself in the activities of others rather than make room for what was important to her.

In time, Michael and Elise found a balance in their work and relational lives. It was not easy, but they are now much happier. The improvement came as a result of changing several things. Michael had to cut back on the number of hours he spent on the job, which turned out to be more difficult than he had imagined. Together they carved out more time to spend together, recreating some of the adventure they shared during their courtship and the early years of their marriage. Elise, on the other hand, had to find pleasure in activities outside of her marriage. She had to rediscover parts of her personality that she had buried long ago. Eventually, she found new interests, such as scrapbooking and meeting for coffee with other mothers of young children. She joined an exercise club and dusted off her bicycle, which had been stored in a corner of the garage for several years. Elise learned that she could not be happy with her marriage until she was happy with herself.

Individuality

Without thinking, many people have accepted the myth that intimacy automatically results when one spends a great deal of time with his or her spouse. In fact, many people believe that the answer to rediscovering intimacy equates to spending more time together. This can be a vital component, but it is not the only ingredient to a healthy marriage. One of the most essential components of a healthy relationship is being a healthy individual.

Having a true connection with others requires that you have a true connection with yourself. This is a foundational truth that you must recognize. When we are alienated from our own experiences, we will be alienated from our spouse. We will have no basis to form a relationship with others. How do we comprise our individuality? Let's explore a few ways.

One of the primary aspects of individuality is *knowing how you feel* about different people, events, and circumstances in your life. You are able to identify your feelings and share them with others. If this is difficult for you, as it is for many people, you may need to practice thinking about how you feel about things and sharing those thoughts with your spouse and other close friends.

A second aspect of individuality is *knowing what you think*. This too is harder than it sounds. How many times have you been asked what you think, and are only able to respond with "I don't know"? You *do* know, of course, but sharing your opinions with others may take work, not to mention a degree of risk.

Another aspect of individuality is *knowing what you want*. Here we get into a bit of your fantasy life. What are your dreams? What would you like from your partner? If you have been obsessed with pleasing people for a long time, you probably expect them to read your mind. They should know what you want without you having to tell them. Unfortunately, this kind of thinking is doomed to fail.

Think of individuality as your own personal space, like a house with a fence around it. Neighborhoods have many houses, but each one's distinguishing features set it off from the others. Different colors, different rooflines and shapes, different landscaping, and other characteristics give each house a unique look. And we wouldn't have it any other way.

Unique characteristics help define your house, but you may still want a fence that separates it from the neighbors'. The fence is an extra measure of protection that keeps people out of your private space unless you give them a special invitation to enter. Without a fence that provides a polite separation between you and other people, they can invade your space. When people invade your space in relationships, they can tell you what to think, what to do, and even how to act. Without this fence, this protective barrier, you will be tempted to please others when to do so will be hurtful to you. Without this fence you become like others, lacking the individuality that sets you apart and contributes to your uniqueness.

Challenges to Individuality

If you have been raised with a pleasing personality, you might not know how you feel, what you think, and what you want. You may be frightened about the prospect of defining how you are different from others. Because of low self-esteem, common among those who live their lives to please others, you may have become enmeshed with your family and your friends. In particular, you may find that you are obsessed with the happiness of your partner. If your spouse is happy, you are happy. If your spouse is sad, you may be sad. After years of being dependent on others for your self-esteem, exerting your individuality can be very intimidating.

Perhaps the greatest deterrent to the individuality necessary for a healthy marriage is the inability to say no. If you are unable to say no or to set boundaries for yourself, then you are unable to prevent people from crashing into your space. You will feel controlled by others when, in fact, your missing boundaries may be setting the stage for you to feel controlled.

People who come to see me for counseling often complain that others don't take them seriously and don't respect their wishes. They point the finger at husbands, mothers-in-law, coworkers, and neighbors, blaming them for the problem. However, the problem usually does not reside with others. It usually resides with the person doing the finger-pointing. It stems from their difficulty to say what they mean. It stems from a fear of setting boundaries and from a willingness to tolerate certain behaviors in others. I tell my clients, "If they are not getting it, you are not giving it to them straight enough. You need to try it again."

If you struggle with low self-esteem and an absence of boundaries, expressing your opinions may be frightening. You will be tempted to tell people what you think they want to hear. In fact, you may already be very skilled at identifying "the right thing to say" because doing so will bring the reward of knowing that you have pleased them. Although they are likely to express their approval of you, you will sacrifice your individuality in the process.

Rebecca was a middle-aged woman who was obviously discouraged when she came for counseling. Since their youngest child had left home, she had been depressed. A mother of three grown children, she suddenly found herself directionless.

Rebecca was a kind woman. She had a quick smile and made every effort to please my staff at the time of her arrival. Rebecca deferred to us and was ingratiating in her conversation. I could easily see that she had spent years attempting to please others.

Her history revealed that she had always put others before herself. She had been married for many years to a man whom she described as controlling. She had invested her life's energies in her children and spouse, and now that the kids were gone, all that was left was to wait on her husband. Suddenly, this was no longer enough to make her happy.

Beneath her deferential style was deep-seated anger. She could not show this openly, however, because doing so would violate how she viewed herself and how she was taught to behave. Her anger emerged in occasional sarcastic comments and unwarranted irritation with herself.

My work with Rebecca was challenging because her patterns of behavior were deeply entrenched. Her personality had developed around the core value of serving others. After many sessions, she came to be more assertive. As her independence grew, she recognized the value of being an individual. She was surprised to see her marriage improve along with her newly discovered self-esteem. Her husband had wanted her to speak up all along and valued her newfound opinions. He was not as controlling as she had once thought.

Still, the transformation was slow and awkward. She would practice her assertiveness at times, only to fall back into passivity. She was also not prepared to deal with conflicts that ensued when she voiced contrary opinions to her husband. She had to work hard to learn that conflict did not mean they were heading for divorce court.

From my perspective, watching the new Rebecca emerge after years of suppressing her thoughts, feelings, and desires was delightful and rewarding.

The Dance of Interdependence

Marriage is obviously not a solo enterprise. For a husband and wife to become so enmeshed that they cannot distinguish where one ends and the other begins is not healthy. In a good marriage, two unique and secure people come together to form a partnership.

If you have been working on being your own person—telling others what you think, feel, and want—being involved with another person may be threatening. This is why understanding the concept of interdependence is necessary. Michael and Elise had to recreate their relationship. They had to talk about what a marriage would look like where each person enjoyed individual activities, but then they came together to form a special friendship. As I indicated earlier, this did not occur without serious birth pains. Elise went through a period of self-doubt and discouragement before finding a way to ask for what she needed without smothering Michael. Michael had to find a way to give more of himself to their marriage while still enjoying the fruits of a career. They sometimes stepped on one another's toes and had to work through hurt feelings and misunderstandings. But because I had explained that this was inevitable, they were not alarmed when it happened.

Michael and Elise learned that interdependence meant

- They would enjoy individual activities.

- These activities would bring fresh energy to their marriage.

- They would have same-sex friends of their own.

- They would have friends that they enjoyed together.

- They were free to disagree with one another.

- They would have different desires, thoughts, and feelings.

- They would build a strong bond together.

Interdependence occurs when individuals with distinct personalities—distinct tastes in food, music, clothing, politics—choose to come together to create a partnership that enhances individuality through the bond of love.

God's View of Marriage

God, of course, is the author of the perfect marriage. Throughout Scripture we see the biblical story woven through the drama of relationships. We will never obtain a perfect relationship, but we can consult the original design as a means of doing the best we can. Let's explore marriage as God intended it. As Larry Crabb says in his book *The Marriage Builder,*

> Within the context of relationship can the deepest needs of human personality be met. People everywhere long for intimate relationships. We all need to be close to someone. Make no apology for your strong desire to be intimate with someone; it is neither sinful nor selfish. Don't ignore the need by preoccupying yourself with peripheral satisfactions such as social achievement or acquiring knowledge. Neglecting your longing for relationship by claiming to be above it is as foolish as pretending you can live without food. Our need for relationship is real, and it is there by God's design.[4]

But how do we answer the questions about interdependence in a marital relationship? How do we understand God when He says couples are to be united with one another and that "they will become one flesh"? (Genesis 2:24). This certainly sounds like they are to become indistinguishable from one another—everything we have cautioned against! Does God want us to surrender our personality to another?

The biblical pattern for marriage takes nothing away from our personality. In fact, marriage as God designed it helps us reach our full potential. Certainly nothing is sweeter than the picture of marriage as God designed it: two people living as one flesh for a lifetime. The apostle Paul recites the words of the Creator in his epistle to the Ephesians, noting that the husband and wife are to become one with each other. He calls marriage a mystery, a label with which many of us would heartily agree! (Ephesians 5:31). But becoming "one flesh" does not mean denying who you are.

Drs. Townsend and Cloud have helped thousands understand a complex principle of human functioning: the importance of setting healthy boundaries in our relationships so that two people can be one and yet distinct. They have helped us see, in their numerous books on the issue of boundaries, that God created an orderly world where boundaries are part of His design. He not only established the universe with boundaries but also designed relationships to have them as well. Drs. Townsend and Cloud clarify this issue in their book *Boundaries in Marriage:*

> Marriage is first and foremost about love. It is bound together by the care, need, companionship, and values of two people, which can overcome hurt, immaturity, and selfishness to form something better than what each person alone can produce. Love is at the heart of marriage, as it is at the heart of God himself (1 John 4:16). Yet, love is not enough. The marriage relationship needs other ingredients to grow and thrive. Those ingredients are *freedom* and *responsibility*. When two people are free to disagree, they are free to love. When they are not free, they live in fear, and love dies: "Perfect love drives out fear" (1 John 4:18). And when two people

together take responsibility to do what is best for the marriage, love can grow. When they do not, one takes on too much responsibility and resents it; the other does not take on enough and becomes self-centered or controlling. Freedom and responsibility problems in a marriage will cause love to struggle.[5]

Thus, with an understanding of the principles of *freedom* and *responsibility*, we see that Rebecca was not being responsible when she became overly passive and gave up her self to become the caretaker of her family. By becoming self-less, she enabled her family to become irresponsible, which is certainly not a part of God's plan. Elise, likewise, was irresponsible with her self. She expected Michael to be everything to her, rather than taking responsibility for her life by maintaining friendships and fulfilling activities of her own. She expected too much from Michael—more than he could give. Fortunately, both came to an awareness of their codependent tendencies in time to make appropriate adjustments. They learned the role that freedom and responsibility play in a sound marriage.

In any healthy relationship, a clear understanding of who is responsible for what is critical. Boundaries are essential for each person to be responsible for his or her own

- feelings
- attitudes
- behaviors
- choices
- limits

- desires
- thoughts
- values
- talents
- love[6]

Two unique individuals build a successful marriage when they come together in the bond of love to create something wonderful that they cannot achieve on their own. In order for this to occur, we must be responsible for our own behavior, not our spouse's.

The Dance of Intimacy

The dance of intimacy is one of closeness, passion, and the occasional sore toe. When you work at being responsible for yourself and not your spouse, conflict will sometimes result. This is a healthy thing and can actually increase the level of trust and intimacy in a healthy relationship.

First, a strong relationship requires two interdependent people, each one responsible for his or her own thoughts and emotions, coming together to form a partnership. One client said it like this: "I have realized that it does no good for me to agree with Jim if I really do not in my heart. He appreciates it if I am honest with him about my feelings and thoughts. He wants me to be me, not a clone of him."

Second, these two people must have their own lives, separate from one another. Consider how boring life would be if two people did the same things, thought the same thoughts, and had the same feelings. This may sound like heaven, but we would soon tire of it. Most of us want someone who adds spice to our lives. They do this by being different, just as God intended. Thus, they will have their own interests, preferences, and feelings.

Third, both people will be relatively secure in themselves, willing to risk sharing differing opinions and emotions. They will be secure enough in themselves to know they do not always need agreement from their partner. They will be secure enough to tolerate tension at times. They will know they cannot control their spouse and that they must not enable irresponsible behaviors from him or her.

Finally, in a healthy marriage both partners are able to share their feelings and thoughts. They have good communication and conflict-resolution skills. In the climate of understanding, they do not strive to think identically but respect the differences and the strengths that come from those differences. They are willing to be vulnerable with each other, sharing their pain as well as their joy.

Perfect Love

Any serious reading of 1 Corinthians 13, perhaps the greatest lesson on love ever written, will leave one breathless. Here we catch a glimpse of perfect love, the kind known only by God. In Paul's words, we see what true love is all about.

> If I speak in the tongues of men and of angels, but have not love, I am only a resounding gong or a clanging symbol. If I have the gift of prophecy and can fathom all mysteries and all knowledge, and if I have a faith that can move mountains, but have not love, I am nothing... Love is patient, love is kind. It does not envy, it does not boast, it is not proud. It is not rude, it is not self-seeking, it is not easily angered, it keeps no record of wrongs. Love does not delight in evil but rejoices with the truth. It always protects, always trusts, always hopes, always perseveres.

This is a humbling passage because it shines its light on all the ways we fall short of perfect love. Yet that light also offers a beacon to guide our way:

- love is patient
- love is kind
- love is not envious
- love is not proud
- love keeps no record of wrongs
- love is not easily angered
- love protects
- love is hopeful
- love perseveres

And the list goes on. This passage clearly shows that we are to be sacrificial in our love. We are to give. But here again, the path can become confusing. We are to give, but we are to be responsible in our giving. We are to care but not to be so obsessive with our caretaking that we enable others to shirk their responsibility. We are to be sacrificial but to take care of ourselves in the process. As we appropriately care for ourselves, we are better able to care for our spouse and others.

We can become either discouraged or encouraged by the principles addressed in this scripture. We are discouraged if we expect that we could adhere to these truths perfectly. We are encouraged if we know that we are lovingly embraced by God as He guides us toward the goal of perfect love.

Paul shares from his heart. "Now we see but a poor reflection as in a mirror; then we shall see face to face. Now I know in part; then I shall know fully, even as I am fully known." Love never fails.

Reflection

Using 1 Corinthians 13 as your guide to perfect love, reflect on the love you are giving. List a few ways you can demonstrate that your love is…

- patient
- kind
- persevering

In what ways will this kind of love strengthen your relationship?

Chapter Five

Controlling
Children

*I value this delicious home feeling as one of the
choicest gifts a parent can bestow.*

WASHINGTON IRVING

"What am I doing up at this awful hour?" Lisa Kaufman
mumbled as the fluorescent light flickered in the kitchen. The clock
read 5:00 A.M. She glanced at the comforting darkness outside and
wished she were back in bed. Fumbling with the coffeemaker, Lisa
hurriedly tried to get some caffeine into her system to ready herself for the flight to Cincinnati. She was beginning to have serious
concerns about the public relations consulting contract she had
signed: *Will it take too much of my time? Will I be able to accomplish
what I promised? Will my girls be okay while I'm gone?*

She and her husband, Gary, have two girls, seven and nine, who
demand lots of attention. Her mind raced as the questions barraged
her sleep-deprived mind: *Did I tell Joey to remember to let the dog
out the next few days? Did I remind Gary to get the girls to gymnas-
tics? Did I remember to call the daycare about Jennifer's special diet?
Did I cancel the orthodontist appointment?* She struggled to stay
focused on her trip, but it was impossible.

After packing lunches for the day and making sure that her bags
were packed for her flight later that morning, she went into the
children's room to rouse them. As she watched them sleep, she

smiled and reflected on the wonder of this moment. How she loved them. She and Gary were not sure they would be able to have children, but now they were blessed with two healthy daughters.

She tapped their shoulders, waking them slowly and carefully. They did not like the morning any more than she did. As Lisa touched Jennifer, she rolled over, groaned, and muttered something about not wanting to get up. Lisa could certainly relate to those sentiments. But she persisted with the morning ritual: coaxing them out of bed, combing tangled hair, hounding them to brush their teeth, arbitrating the arguments over what clothes they would wear, nagging them to eat their breakfast, hurrying them off to the school bus. Four hours of work packed into one, she thought, and her day was just beginning.

Gary had pressures of his own. He would be up in half an hour, ready to climb onto the treadmill of his day. His mind would not be on the kids but on the challenges of his job as editor of the local newspaper. While he was supportive of Lisa, he did very little to help out. His focus was limited to his job and the demands of being a church elder.

In a few minutes, the Kaufman family would be darting about like traffic at a busy intersection. Four people, four sets of emotions, and four directions—with Lisa wearing the badge and whistle to keep the traffic moving. Because she wanted to offer her children every possible advantage in life, she maintained a frantic pace taking them to their dance classes, soccer practices, and piano lessons. Lisa's thoughts always raced, scanning the mental list that directed her energies:

- children's needs

- job expectations

- marriage

- church commitments

- and more

Demands, expectations, more demands. A husband that wanted her to care for their children, and children that expected her to be supermom. Would it ever end, she wondered? But Lisa was inadvertently teaching them to rely completely and solely on her. She received little if any appreciation for the job she did managing the family. At times, she felt like she would fly into a million pieces. But then she remembered that she was choosing to work, almost as a respite from the grind at home. She felt guilty for dividing her attentions and energies, and so she gave even more time to her children.

Carrie

A peek into Carrie's morning revealed a different scenario. Like Lisa, Carrie was also up at the crack of dawn preparing her family for another day. She was a single mother with three children: a son in high school, a daughter in junior high, and a younger daughter in elementary school. She and her ex-husband had spread out the children's births in an effort to more effectively manage their family.

Carrie was a doting mother. She had deliberately postponed her graduate school education and career in order to be home with the children. She and her ex-husband had agreed that this arrangement would be best for the kids. After all, kids need a parent in the home to get them off to school and greet them when they get home.

Carrie had not been in favor of the divorce. It had taken its emotional toll. Her ex-husband, Kelly, had insisted on it as he said that he no longer loved her. Now she had to reconsider her options. She resented being a single mother facing financial pressures in addition to being the sole caregiver for three children. Kelly provided little beyond the compulsory child support. Still, Carrie enjoyed the role of mother. If only she could do it freely, without pressure, as she and Kelly had originally planned. Now she had to make other arrangements. She decided to finish her education and prepare to earn a livable income.

The house was quiet until the first alarm went off. It was followed by the beeping of a second alarm and blaring music in another bedroom. Then came an eruption of clatter. Her children were able to get up on their own, but that is where their responsibility seemed to stop. Moments later the screaming began.

"Mom!" her oldest son, Sean, yelled. "Where's that shirt you washed for me yesterday?" She could hear him muttering to himself as he dug through his closet.

"Mom!" her youngest daughter, Beth, yelled minutes later. "I told you I wanted a tuna fish sandwich. I'm not eating peanut butter again. I hate this stuff!" Carrie heard the refrigerator door slam shut, and she headed to the kitchen to see if they had any tuna.

Meanwhile, she could hear her middle daughter crying in her bedroom. *What in the world is wrong, Chelsea?* Carrie wondered as she opened Chelsea's bedroom door. "Why aren't you getting ready for school?"

"Look at my stupid face," Chelsea cried. "I'm not going to school looking like this. I have zits all over the place. Why didn't you buy me that cream I asked for? I can't believe you forgot."

In spite of the chaos, Carrie was like a calm field general in the midst of battle. She was able to approach each child with composure. She listened carefully to their complaints and offered answers that they sometimes accepted and sometimes did not. She was often able to anticipate what might be troubling her children and provide solutions. Like Lisa, Carrie would jump to meet her children's needs, striving to be the perfect mother.

At last, all three children were out the door. Carrie breathed a sigh of relief. She was tempted to sit down and rest, but she knew that her day was just beginning. She glanced at the Bible sitting on the coffee table, wondering if she could squeeze in a little time for study. But she had to be in class in an hour and needed to complete her other reading so that she would be prepared.

The Queen of Guilt

In spite of all Lisa and Carrie did for their children, rarely did they feel as if their efforts were enough. They always had a nagging sense that something had been left undone. Recently I heard a client of mine say that she felt that mothers automatically received the title Queen of Guilt upon the birth of a child. Like a rite of passage, it is bestowed upon mothers from their mothers, who received it from their mothers. All that is missing is the scepter and tiara.

Do you ever feel like the Queen of Guilt? The title comes with many responsibilities, most noticeably an irritating feeling that you are never doing enough. And so you become a "human doing" rather than a "human being." Your worth comes from outside rather than from within. You look at your family and invariably question whether you are doing enough. You look at your children and take personal responsibility for every nick and scratch they suffer. You watch, look, and listen to see how they are faring, giving little thought to how you are feeling and doing. If they are well, you are well. If not, you feel inadequate. And so it is with many mothers.

The Queen of Guilt has an overactive conscience, probably stemming from some of the childhood issues that we have previously discussed. Look at the job title a bit closer. These women are responsible for making sure…

- everyone in the family is happy
- everyone's needs are met
- the children are perfectly healthy
- the meals are balanced
- the home is well kept
- the finances are stable
- the social arrangements are made

And the list goes on. Take a moment to consider what else you would add to this never-ending inventory of responsibilities.

Something is engaging about the role and the rights that come with the title. That's why you keep the position, right? If the honorary designation, Queen of Guilt, had no payoffs, you would give it up in a heartbeat. But the payoffs are real. The Queen of Guilt is entitled to

- feel exhausted and unappreciated (martyr)

- have the last word

- be irritable and moody

- dictate how things will be done

- be looked to for answers

As you can see, the benefits may not exceed the burdens. However, for some people, the attention they receive is worth the suffering. If you have struggled with self-esteem issues, you may have unconsciously decided that some recognition and royalty is better than none. Now is the time to reexamine the job and decide if you want to offer your resignation.

Creating the Perfect Family

Many women run their families with the precision of a drill sergeant at boot camp. They have taken on the responsibility of managing their homes, their children, and sometimes even their husbands. These items constitute their turf, and they are very protective of it. Many have become grand caretakers—the consummate leaders of the troops.

Often because of a childhood of turmoil, those who are anxious about pleasing others try to be perfect. They attempt to create the ideal family. They notice everyone's feelings but their own. They are externally focused and become anxious when anyone in the family is unhappy. At the first sign of distress, they work to make everyone feel better. Of course, this plan is doomed to failure. Perfect people and perfect families do not exist. In fact, all families have dysfunctional qualities to some degree. God gave us a model for perfect family functioning, but the Bible clearly states that we will never be perfect (1 John 1:10). That is why we need God in our lives.

Like many mothers, Lisa and Carrie are obsessed with trying to please everyone in the family. They feel as if they should be able to solve any problem that arises. No situation should be outside of their control. If we stand aside and observe, we will see them slowly wearing down. We know that they will end up frustrated, angry, and exhausted. At some point, they may develop physical symptoms that signal an end to their bodies' reserves. We watch as they frantically meet need after need. We want to scream, "Stop!" but we know that they will stop only if they find a better way to live.

In the *Love Is a Choice Workbook*, we read,

> Codependents struggle through life like a car running on the fumes, sputtering its way to the gas station. The messages of worth and dignity they missed in their childhood have left a big empty space. In despair they look outside themselves to find meaning and purpose in life.[1]

Women often look to their families to provide them with the sense of well-being that they have been unable to find within themselves. Women like Lisa and Carrie want their children to think they have the perfect mother. They will go out of their way to keep their children happy, buying them the latest fashions and CDs, running them to ball games and movies, doing whatever is necessary to be seen as the best mother possible. The problem is that the only way Lisa and Carrie can gain happiness is in the role of the perfect mother.

When the precarious balance between self and family tips too far in one direction, problems result for both mother and children.

Excessive Dependence upon Children

People pleasers need to be needed. While their children rely on them for everything imaginable, these mothers desperately need their children to need them. Thus, they create an excessive dependency upon their own children.

Robin Norwood, bestselling author of *Women Who Love Too Much*, suggests that many women continue in the roles they learned as children.

> For many women who love too much, those roles often meant that we denied our own needs while trying to meet the needs of other family members. Perhaps we were forced by circumstances to grow up too fast, prematurely taking on adult responsibilities because our mother or father was too sick physically or emotionally to carry out the appropriate parental functions. When this happened, we learned too young and too well how to take care of everyone but ourselves. Our own needs for love, attention, nurturing, and security went unmet while we pretended to be more powerful and less fearful, more grown-up and less needy, than we really felt. And, having learned to deny our own yearning to be taken care of, we grew up looking for more opportunities to do what we had become so good at: being preoccupied with someone else's wants and demands rather than acknowledging our own fear and pain and unmet needs.[2]

People pleasers have many unmet needs. One way to meet those needs is by causing others to depend upon them. What better place to act this out than with their children, who have no end to their needs?

Lisa acts exasperated with her role as mother and public relations consultant. If the truth be known, she wouldn't have it any other way. While she may mutter about her husband's failure to provide help at home, she has an underlying need to be all things to all people. She has an excessive dependency upon her children that typically goes unobserved. She depends upon her children to depend upon her. She will change when she becomes so exhausted that she has no other choice than to take better care of herself.

The Paradox of Control

As if this whole situation is not confusing enough, let's look at it through yet another lens. Note this paradox: That which we try to control ends up controlling us. Let's look closer at Carrie's life to help us understand this principle.

We can easily see how Carrie could succumb to being a people pleaser. She became a single mother under painful circumstances. Her husband left in spite of her protests and willingness to seek counsel. She could not make him stay and work on their relationship. She could, however, regain a degree of control and self-worth by investing herself completely in the lives of her children. Carrie felt tremendous guilt for the demise of her marriage. While she did not do anything heinous to cause it, she was distraught that she was powerless to fix the relationship. She watched as the children cried over the loss of their father. She watched as her children grieved and became angry when their father did not stay involved in their lives as he had promised. No matter how hard she tried, she could not shield them from the pain of the divorce. Silently, she vowed to do whatever was necessary to make it up to them.

Carrie decided to try to be everything to her children. She tried to eliminate every situation that might cause them pain; they'd had enough for a lifetime, she reasoned. As she worked overtime to alleviate their pain, their whims began to control her. Continuing to treat them as wounded infants would not help them heal and grow into healthy adults. The pain she tried to control ended up controlling her.

Recently my heart went out to a young woman who found herself unprepared for the rigors of being a stepparent. Tracy was just 30 years old and already was trying to raise her husband's adolescent son and daughter from a previous marriage. With no children of her own and no experience being a mother, she suddenly inherited the full-time job of raising a 14-year-old stepdaughter and 13-year-old stepson. She and her husband, Bill, sat before me with their marriage obviously in trouble.

Before she even began sharing her experience, I could see the tension on her face. She appeared tired and said she had lost weight over the past year. She glared at her husband who returned her piercing stares. I asked them to share what had taken place. She told the following story.

"When we were dating, Bill told me that we would raise the kids together. He wanted me involved and understood my style of discipline. He even told the kids that I would have authority when they were in our home. Well, that all changed when they came to live with us. Now they don't listen to me, and he won't support me when I discipline them."

I certainly could empathize with her situation. She was being asked to step into a ready-made family and act as a parent without the history needed to really parent these children. I asked Bill to share his perspective.

"I was serious when I told Tracy that I wanted her to be a mother to my kids. But they have been raised a certain way and are not used to her style of parenting. I wasn't ready for the uproar that took place when she tried to step in. I have my kids coming to me all the time telling me that she is being too harsh and that they don't like her. I'm caught in the middle."

Tracy stood up at this point and began to pace.

"I can't stand to hear this stuff," she said. "His kids need to listen to me. He lets them get away with murder, and I won't stand for it in my home. They need to toe the line. That's the way I want to run things in my home. He has to support me."

"But, Tracy," Bill blurted. "I have never parented the kids the way you want to parent them. You want to have complete control, and they are not going to respect you. Can't you see that? The harder you push them, the more they are going to rebel."

"Tracy, I think Bill has given you something to think about," I said. "The more you try to control these kids, the more they are going to push you away. I think you need to back off a little and develop a healthy relationship with them, and then Bill will be able to support you more in your role as stepmother."

"That's going to be really hard for me," she said. "I'm used to doing things a certain way. They really make me mad. But I do see that my way is not working."

After several sessions, Tracy could see more clearly that trying to exert control over a situation where she had little power was useless and counterproductive. Trying to control those things that we cannot control, which is one of the chief symptoms of code-pendency, only makes us irritable and angry. It is a waste of energy that is better spent learning how to effectively care for ourselves.

Manipulating Children

What is the result when a mother dedicates her life to making sure that her children experience no pain? What happens when they can sense that she needs them to need her? The result is children who carry their mother's pain. In addition, they know that they can manipulate her to do for them what they could do for themselves.

Sadly, we see this pattern in children of all ages. For example, many grown children that continue to manipulate their parents to get what they want. They want their mother's approval, and they know that one way to get it is to be needy. While their mother may sometimes balk at dealing with this neediness, particularly in the case of adult children, both have colluded for so long that they accept this arrangement.

Let's look at Carrie's life again. Her three children know that when they yell, scream, pout, and misbehave, she will come running. Mom wants to solve problems, and her kids have plenty of them. The tragedy is that they will not learn to solve problems on their own. They will constantly look to their mother to clean up their messes.

I am reminded of a mature, professional couple that had three children—two in college and one a recent graduate. The couple had planned and sacrificed for many years to create the opportunity for their children to attend private universities. The parents were rightfully proud of their children's academic accomplishments. However, tension began developing after the oldest son graduated.

This couple came to see me after a long spell of fighting about how long to subsidize their son after graduation. The mother wanted to take care of him "until he could get his feet on the ground." The father felt that their son was ready to be self-sufficient. Six months after graduation, their son still had no job prospects in sight. While the parents paid for his apartment and food bills, he spent his time partying and catching up on pleasure reading he hadn't been able to do while in college.

To complicate matters, their son was a genuinely nice guy. Both parents agreed that their son was a well-adjusted youth who was law-abiding, spiritually grounded, and a pleasure to have around.

Indeed, he sounded like a fine young man who simply did not want to hurry into the adult world of work.

This scenario, to varying degrees, is repeated in many homes across America. Young people have a natural tendency to postpone working until absolutely necessary. And if their parents are willing to pay the bills, this grace period may be extended far too long. Unfortunately, parents who allow this pattern to become established run the risk of creating learned helplessness in their children. The more children rely on their parents, the less they accept responsibility for their own lives.

This couple came to see me for several months, arguing their points vehemently. The mother clearly needed to be a caretaker for her son. She was reluctant to give up her deeply established role as mother and needed her son to remain a child a bit longer. Eventually she came to see that treating her son as an infant only allowed him to be manipulative, which was clearly not in his best interests. Moreover, it prevented her from creating a healthy, adult identity for herself apart from being a mother. Her world had become so narrow that it was limited to caring for her children. She needed to expand her horizons and make the adjustment from having dependent children to being on a more equal basis with them. This is ultimately the task of all parents.

Lost in the Shuffle

When you settle into the role of homemaker, wife, and mother, you can easily become lost in the shuffle. It can happen so subtly that you might not even see it happening. You wake up one day and realize that you feel lost. Perhaps this feeling caused you to pick up this book. That's good. Awareness of being lost is the first step to finding your way again. Let's consider some of the effects of being lost.

Lost from Your Husband

I doubt that I have to remind you that if you spend all of your energies outside of yourself, you cannot truly be available to your spouse. You know that feeling of plopping into bed at night, thoroughly exhausted and angry that he would have the audacity to ask for sexual relations. You know the irritation you feel when he presses in upon you with that request.

But let me remind you that you have a responsibility to your spouse. Since you have chosen to be married, you must give important energy to your relationship. You can deny this fact for a while, but ultimately, you will damage the intimacy of your marriage if you ignore it. And you can only attend to it if you have some emotional reserves.

Paying attention to your marriage is, however, not to be equated with losing yourself in the marriage. I hope we have dispelled that myth. Two complete individuals are necessary to create one flesh. If you do not take care of yourself, you cannot be emotionally available to him.

Lost from Your Children

We have spent this chapter talking about giving too much of yourself to your children. We have discussed losing yourself in the role of mother. However, this is quite different from giving yourself in a healthy way to the role of motherhood.

Healthy mothering means letting your kids learn from their mistakes. It means *not* being there to pick up all the pieces, knowing that they will be all right without your constant vigilance. It means giving them the message that they are important to you but letting them know that you have other responsibilities to other people and to yourself. You have a life apart from your children.

Proper modeling will have a tremendous impact upon your children. As they watch you live a healthy and balanced life, they will benefit accordingly. You will be teaching them a very important lesson when you say, "Please do not interrupt me unless it is an emergency. I am not available for the next hour. I am going to take a long, hot bath."

You will be offering them an invaluable experience when you say, "I am not going to step into this fight you are having with your sister. I know you two can work it out."

You will be showing confidence in their problem-solving abilities when you say, "I know that you will figure out how to raise your grades. I am willing to talk with your teacher to develop a plan, but I am not willing to watch over your shoulder while you do your homework."

You can see the fine line between caring and caretaking. When you find it, you will feel much better, and your children will gain independence.

Lost from Your Family

As we reflect upon the lives of Lisa and Carrie, we can see that they cannot possibly develop healthy, functional relationships with their children until significant changes are made. This is not to say that everything about those relationships is dysfunctional. But as these women scurry about trying to be everything to everyone, rarely bothering to attend to their personal needs, they will soon be running on empty.

Families are living, breathing entities of their own making. Consider how each family has its own unique fingerprint, history, rituals, goals, and desires. God designed the family to be that special place for each individual to find significance and security. That does not always happen, as we know. But by taking care of yourself, you can break the cycle of codependency. You can teach your children and your husband that your needs must also be met.

Lost from Your Heavenly Father

The Scriptures tell us that we were fearfully and wonderfully made by our Creator (Psalm 139:14). God loves us so much that He has given us a special place in all of creation. We know that He desires to be a part of our lives. That is not possible if we spend every waking moment pleasing others at our own expense.

Consider what is required to maintain a healthy relationship. Think about the energies you expend on your closest friendship. Think about the most important person to you and how you feel about having him or her in your heart. Your heavenly Father wants that kind of relationship with you as well—not out of obligation but because He longs to be with you. Finding the time and energy to build your life on Him is essential.

Lost from Yourself

Finally, let's reflect upon how easily you can become lost from yourself when giving all of your energy to your children. Your children are worthy of your dearest attention and affections, but you must reserve time for you.

I ask that you make a commitment to rediscover yourself. You have not picked up this book by accident, nor are you likely to be reading it for pleasure. You are probably reading it because you have become lost from yourself. You will do others in your life a great favor by taking time to understand what you feel, think, and want. This will involve listening to what God is asking of you as well, for this is a crucial aspect of your identity.

I am convinced that within each person a personal quest is taking place. God gives each of us a personal mission. He created us to do good works (Ephesians 2:10). He has given each of us unique and strategic gifts, all with the purpose of serving and edifying others in the body of Christ (Romans 12:3-8). We feel a "burden" at times as we are considerate of the needs, doubts, and fears of others

(Romans 15:2). But this burden, far from being an excessive expenditure of our energy for the purpose of pleasing others, becomes an expression of our desire to fulfill our unique mission of helping others become mature and Christlike. Take the time necessary to let this gifting give birth to whatever God wants to do in, and with, your life.

The Healthy Mother

Sarah was a young woman with a husband and three children. She was full of energy but had a calm presence. She dressed simply. What struck me was her clear sense of purpose. She was leading a retreat on "call" and the purpose of God in your life. Her voice was firm. She was certain about what she was saying. When she spoke, she looked straight into my eyes with no fear of genuine contact.

I met her several years ago at a weekend retreat on "Understanding Your Call" at a Catholic abbey. I hadn't been to this place before. Nestled in the woods, it was a bit frightening. It had no phones, no television, none of the customary artifacts that fill my life. I was only miles from home yet light-years away.

Sarah led the retreat quietly and with style. She told us about her transition in life from a single career woman to a mother with three small children. At first, she said, she felt that she had lost her direction in life. She had been pursuing a professional track and then felt called to become married and raise a family, seeing her home as a place for God to utilize her gifts and fulfill His mission. The transition was confusing for her.

At first, she said, she struggled to find space for God amid the hustle and bustle of family life. She had lost herself for a time in raising her children. Her personal quiet time was easily eaten up with the clamoring cries of her children. She had to work through periods of questioning and self-reflection, and even now she did not feel that she had "arrived." She cautioned us against finding overly simple solutions to the challenges of life.

She spoke of her intention to create space for God in the everyday movement of life, not in some imaginary place that we think life ought to be. We need to create a place, she said, where we can listen to what He might ask of us. She spoke of God wanting the best for us, wanting to give to us. She spoke of grace. She reminded us of the words of Thomas Merton, that the greatest violence that we do to ourselves is in not creating time and space to simply "be."

In some ways, Sarah reminded me of a younger version of my own mother, who is now in her eighties. Once robust and full of the vigor necessary to raise five children, my mother now walks slowly and with assistance from my doting father. They are more in love today than at any other time in their lives. Seeing them together is sheer delight. My mother retains the solid thinking of the elementary teacher she was for many years, but she is now more reflective. She accepts fewer certainties and more imponderables. She is more available. She has the time and the inclination to truly be present to each of us and to listen closely to what God may be calling her to do even at this stage of life. She exudes the delight that comes from paying attention to God's mysterious beckoning. She remains, even now, a mother to her children, inviting us with her genuine hospitality and acceptance, her gifts to us.

So what is a healthy mother? She is a person who can discern the needs of those in her care while also being present to herself. She understands that she must know her own heart and mind in order to be fully available to others. She listens carefully to how God is ever calling her forward in her unique mission and purpose. She maintains clear boundaries about what she is responsible for and what she is not. She manages her roles appropriately without neglecting any of them or obsessing over any of them. She models a strong, loving relationship with her husband. She expects her children to behave responsibly and knows that they must contribute to the family as well as receive from it. With healthy boundaries and insight given by God, you can become this kind of person.

"She speaks with wisdom, and faithful instruction is on her tongue" (Proverbs 31:26).

Reflection

Are you moving through life like a car running on fumes? Consider your relationship with each person listed below. Are you ignoring any? Are you enjoying each one?

- your spouse
- your children
- your self
- your heavenly Father

Consider how you might establish a healthier relationship with each person listed above.

Chapter Six

Creating a Healthy Family

*Your real home is in this place.
At this time. The present is for action,
for doing, for becoming, and for growing.*

DAVID VISCOTT

I awakened slowly, wiping the sleep from my eyes. I could hear my mom bustling about in the kitchen while the rest of the house remained quiet. My two younger sisters were still sleeping. My dad was undoubtedly outside readying his boat for a fishing excursion in the bay. It was mid-morning but there was no rush to get out of bed. Thank goodness for Saturdays—no school.

As I began to clear the fog from my brain, I felt peaceful. I pulled the heavy homemade quilt over my head for a few more minutes of sleep and a chance to mull over how I wanted to spend my day. I liked the weight of the blanket on my body. I was in no hurry, enjoying the chance to let the day unfold naturally, unhurried, unlike the other days of the week that were a blur of activity with kids heading to school, my mother leaving early for her teaching position, and Dad heading to the office. No, this morning the family would move at a slower pace, each of us with our own thoughts, our own plans. Each person was distinct, yet we were a cohesive group. Mom would be calling us together soon for a late breakfast. I was ten years old.

I grew up in an idyllic neighborhood where 15 "mothers" all watched out for "Davey." In fact, to this day they refer to me by my childhood name. The mothers all knew my siblings and me, and my mother knew their children as well. That kind of safety is rare in today's world. But that was my world: Nevada Street in a small town in northwest Washington.

Every weekend was an adventure. Was it a day for baseball, or perhaps a little frog hunting in the "back 40"? We could always spy on the golfers at the local golf course from the safety of a hidden spot in the forest. Or we could hitch a ride to the lake and swim.

When deciding which neighborhood buddy to call to join me, the families often played a role. These families molded my friends' lives. Although I was too young to fully understand these influences, I was beginning to make decisions based upon what I saw when I peered in their front doors. I watched to see if my friends were able to be distinct, if their parents listened to them and understood them. I watched to see if their siblings respected them and honored their boundaries. Some of them were required to be seen and not heard, to be silent and lost in the chaos of their family. I could tell that those who were respected felt good about their families and themselves; conversely, those who were overly controlled felt belittled and hurt.

I came to realize that some families were inviting, open, welcoming. I knew that if I knocked on their door, they would offer me a cookie and some friendly teasing. Others were more foreboding. I found that the emotional tone of a family remained constant over time. Each greeting was similar to the one before. Each visit seemed the same—the same furniture, the same people, the same feeling.

One of my best friends, Tommy, was an only child. Most of my friends had four or five siblings, so having none was an oddity. I wondered what it would be like not having an older brother and sister who picked on me, or not to have two younger sisters who delighted in bugging me. I wanted to ask him why his parents didn't have more children, but that seemed insensitive. I later learned that he was adopted, which created even more questions in my mind. During times of frustration I even wondered if I was adopted.

And what would it be like, I wondered, to live in Johnny's family, who lived next door? He had one older brother, who was much taller and stronger. Johnny was no match for him. His older brother pushed him around and treated him like a nuisance. Johnny tried many different ways to get even, if not with brawn, then with brains.

I watched siblings jockey for position in their families. What interested me most was the emotional tone. I wanted to know how people treated each other in each family. How connected were they to one another? Were they encouraged to foster their individual gifts?

I watched as the grown-ups scurried about the house. I paid attention to how they talked to me. Some of the parents were warm, friendly, and inviting. Others treated me as an interruption. And I watched how they treated their children—my friends. Sometimes the treatment was loving, attentive, caring. Other times it was distant, disengaged, critical. I felt sorry for friends who had fathers that appeared to be angry and demanding, or mothers who were overly concerned and excessively protective.

One father in particular scared me: Mr. Hansen, Tommy's father. He was, in the eyes of a kid, tough and gruff. He rarely smiled. I couldn't understand that because my own father was usually joking and friendly.

I would walk up to the Hansen's house very tentatively and cautiously ring the doorbell as if there were a right and wrong way to do so. Then I waited anxiously for the tall, bearded man to open the door and glare down at me as if I were an unwanted solicitor. I wanted to say, "I come in peace. I just want to play with your son."

"Is Tommy here?" I would ask meekly.

He never answered. Instead he hollered out, "Tommy, it's for you!"

Tommy would come to the door and greet me enthusiastically. He was a great friend. "C'mon in, Davey." I usually followed him to his room to see his newest batch of baseball cards or the latest Elvis album. I often looked around the house, watching for his parents. His mom sometimes appeared in the doorway and said, "Hello, Davey," but his dad had always disappeared.

I couldn't help but sense that Tommy's father cast a pall over the house. Even as a child, I realized that this man was unhappy about something, though I had no idea what might be bothering him. Now I can see that he was probably depressed. I wondered how Mrs. Hansen could tolerate her husband's moodiness. Did they have a loving relationship that I never saw? I wanted to ask Tommy about this but didn't want to invade his privacy or stir up bad feelings in him. He never complained about his father. I never heard him talk about him at all.

Another neighbor's home was quite different. The Jamisons lived in an unfinished house right next door. They always seemed to be in the process of trying to complete it. But while their house was a bit chaotic, their home was not. Mr. and Mrs. Jamison shared an obvious intimacy, and Mrs. Jamison and my mom seemed to be best friends. They always shared coffee together. The Jamisons had an open door policy. They made sure I knew that I never needed to knock. If someone was home, I was supposed to walk in. In fact, they gave me a good-natured scolding if I sat outside waiting for someone to come to the door. I was free to go straight to Donald's room to see if he was working on a model or if the train set was up and running.

In the Jamisons' home I found the same warmth that I felt in my own. The tone was far different than at Tommy's house. Donald's parents allowed him the freedom appropriate for his age. They encouraged him and his brothers in their various pursuits. They spoke directly to their children and to me. Their family seemed warm and inviting. This was a safe place to learn new things, grow emotionally and spiritually, and enjoy the protection of family.

And that is the question each family must inevitably face. How well does each family member encourage the others to develop the unique individuality that God intended for them? Let's explore some of the factors that go into this process.

Family Dynamics

As I discovered growing up as a youngster on Nevada Street, families come in all different sizes, shapes, and colors. But the most important ingredient is character. Each family, in its own way, either succeeded or failed to encourage their children to grow up to be strong and confident, to have a voice in the family, and to learn to lean on one another in a healthy way. Remember that our goal is to find that precarious healthy interdependence that lies somewhere between independence and dependence.

The Scriptures describe the church as a body, and we can apply this useful picture to families as well. "Just as each of us has one body with many members, and these members do not all have the same function, so in Christ we who are many form one body, and each member belongs to all the others" (Romans 12:4-5). Here is a wonderful picture of unity amid diversity. Paul continues this theme in his letter to the Corinthians.

> The body is a unit, though it is made up of many parts; and though all its parts are many, they form one body... Now the body is not made up of one part but of many. If the foot should say, "Because I am not a hand, I do not belong to the body," it would not for that reason cease to be part of the body...But in fact God has arranged the parts in the body, every one of them, just as he wanted them to be (1 Corinthians 12:12-18).

Here we see a beautiful illustration of the importance of every person. Each fulfills a different but critical function in the family. Paul uses an absurd argument to make his point. If each person in the body were an eye, how could we function? If each were a foot, how would we function? But his illustration has a ring of truth to it because he tells us to appreciate the unique gifts of each member. A fundamental truth of the church and human families is that each person is valuable and significant.

This model for family functioning is our ideal; however, it is not always the reality. We live in a world filled with dysfunctional families and unhealthy individuals. Let's examine more closely how families either succeed or fail to create a climate for healthy individuals.

Open and Closed Families

A healthy family provides an atmosphere of warmth and safety. Secrets are few, if they exist at all. No topic is off limits. These homes are warm, and the communication is open. Children know they are loved and valuable. Their parents seek out their opinions and care about their well-being. The parents do not view the children as "small adults" who can fend for themselves. Rather, they receive them as gifts, blessings that need nurturance in order to grow into healthy adults. They are never obligated to "be seen and not heard." Children are free to make noise while having fun, which is only natural. They can have friends over because good parents know that developing social skills is important. These are avenues for creating self-esteem in young people.

And the children in healthy families care about the adults. The children interact with their parents easily. The friendliness and attachment is readily apparent. The family members are sensitive to one another. They express their caring with the occasional touch, with questions that keep them up-to-date with each other, and with teasing that creates warmth and fondness, not shame or ridicule.

In contrast, the closed family has many secrets. In her popular book *Another Chance*, Sharon Wegscheider-Cruse tells us that in many families

> there are certain subjects that have to be treated as if they simply did not exist. Sex, illegitimacy, how much money Dad earns or how he earns it, quarreling between the parents, religious doubts, and certainly abuse of alcohol or drugs are all taboo subjects in many families. In others it may be silently forbidden to imply that Dad (or Mom, if she is the authority figure) ever makes a mistake.[1]

Wegscheider-Cruse goes on to say that families that don't talk about certain topics also generally don't share their feelings. This is particularly true if the feelings are "bad," such as anger, frustration, discouragement, sadness, or fear. The silencing of feelings is a tragic issue in many families. Children who have not learned how to share their feelings are separated from one another and from themselves.

The tragedy does not end here. When sharing feelings is against the rules and certain topics are taboo, members become walled off from one another. They cannot interact openly in an easy, healthy manner. Wegscheider-Cruse says, "Information and feelings stay bottled up inside each one to be handled alone. And since no one has a full and reliable picture of the situation in the family at any given moment, he must speak, act, and make decisions out of ignorance."[2]

Julia was a woman in her fifties who came to see me about her desire to learn more about her feelings. She was experiencing no immediate crisis, but she felt a vague sense of unhappiness and wondered if she was losing her normally happy disposition. Although she came ostensibly because she was unhappy with her job and stressed out in her role as a nurse at our local hospital, she was out of touch with many aspects of her personality. She had gone through life unsure of how she felt about many things.

"I should be happy with my job. It pays me well. I have flexible hours and a prestigious position. I have spent twenty-five years of my life getting to this place, and now I can't seem to be happy there."

"When do you remember starting to feel unhappy?" I asked.

"It seems like it's just gotten a little worse each year. I guess I started complaining to my husband about two years ago. He has been very supportive through the whole thing."

"So, tell me more about your job. What do you find stressful about it?"

She paused for a moment to reflect upon the question. She sat rigidly in the chair. After a few moments she answered.

"I'm not sure that I even like nursing anymore. But I hate to have those thoughts. I've put a lot of time into this profession. Quitting is unthinkable. Changing careers is not an option. I have to learn to like it again. That's all there is to it."

"I don't know that you have to think about changing careers. But I do think that you might want to spend more time reflecting on what you like and dislike about your job. Maybe we can find ways to make work more enjoyable."

"I've never been the kind of person to do much reflecting. I figure that this is the path I've chosen, and I need to make the best of it."

Julia stayed in counseling for several months. As our sessions progressed, she got around to telling me about a childhood in which sharing her feelings was taboo. Her father, who was very strict, decided early on that she and her siblings would become professionals. Her secret desire to pursue the arts did not matter. Because her father was a physician and her mother was a financial analyst, they frowned upon certain professions as being frivolous and impractical. They did not model an open expression of feelings, and Julia readily admitted to having difficulty understanding her feelings.

Counseling was her first opportunity to explore other aspects of herself, including her own happiness, which she had forbidden herself to think about. Ultimately, after months of thoughtful consideration and a great deal of support from her husband, she decided to cut back at work and take some evening art classes. She is not sure where this path will lead, but she feels a great deal of relief simply from allowing herself to explore possibilities.

Engaged and Disengaged Families

A quick walk through many homes will reveal how attached and engaged family members are with one another. The open, engaging home has been designed with children in mind. Kids aren't afraid of making noise or fearful of touching certain objects. This home will show the occasional scratch in the furniture, and at times objects will even get broken. But the unspoken rule is that things can be replaced; children are only on loan for a short time.

Mealtime was important in my home. It was clearly a time to connect with one another. My mother, a full-blooded Swede, made enough food to feed an army. Her message to us was that we were going to sit down and talk to each other. We were going to pause long enough from our individual pursuits to be a family. And Dad enforced her intentions. We were expected to be at the table at mealtime, and few excuses were solid enough to warrant being away. We were an engaged, caring family, and I have tried to pass along those values to my children.

Don't get me wrong. With four siblings, two older and two younger, this was not always a warm, touchy-feely session. My older brother made perfectly clear that I was a nuisance in his life, just as I did to my younger sisters. My older sister and I vacillated back and forth between enjoying each other's company and going our separate ways. But all of us knew, beneath the daily family struggles, that we felt a great deal of warmth and affection for one another. We knew we could count on each other in times of trouble.

Unfortunately, far too many families are disengaged. I always felt sorry for Jimmy. He never complained about his family, though I knew that things were not quite right. His family was disengaged. His parents and siblings went their own way. They didn't gather in the kitchen to talk about their plans for the day. In fact, they had no gathering place at all. The situation with Tommy was even more distressing: He preferred to be at my house; I feared going over to his.

Our other neighbors, the family with the mother who came to our house for coffee with my mom, were clearly engaged and attached to each other. I loved going over to Donald's house. The family hung out in the kitchen and living room. His mom always seemed to have some blackberry pie ready for us. Whenever I showed up, she got out the plates and everyone indulged in heated pie and ice cream.

Can you remember how the families in the neighborhood you grew up in made you feel? Do you remember the homes that seemed to cry out, "Come on in!"? And do you remember those that seemed to warn, "Beware. This is not a friendly place"? Keep the positive examples in mind as we consider healthy boundaries in families.

Enmeshed Families

Families, fellow church members, coworkers, friends, and acquaintances of all types are capable of damaging individuality. Families can be too distant and detached from one another, but they can also be too close. It may be hard to picture too much closeness, but closeness can be stifling. When individuals are too bent on pleasing one another, healthy engagement gives way to unhealthy *enmeshment.*

- Each person has to know what the others are doing.
- No privacy and no appropriate secrets are permitted.
- Gossip is rampant.
- People tell one another how to behave and feel.
- People talk for one another.
- People tell others how the others are feeling or what they are thinking.
- One or more family members is overly controlling.
- The family has a "right" way to do things and no other way is tolerated.

Thankfully, we can learn from scriptural stories of people living out family problems. We even have a biblical account of enmeshment that can help us understand this concept. In the story of Isaac and his sons, Jacob and Esau, we see this principle at work. In his book *Secrets of Your Family Tree*, Dave Carder points out how Isaac was enmeshed with his sons. [3]

As the story unfolds, Carder explains how Isaac showed favoritism to Esau. Isaac turned away from the child God chose, Jacob, in favor of Esau. Their father-son relationship took a turn toward dysfunction, taking on that quality of enmeshment we see in many families today. Esau lost his own identity in favor of becoming what his father wanted him to be. "Esau had a bent to be and do all that Isaac had never been able to do," Carder says. "Here was a chance for Isaac to vicariously become 'a man's man'…Now perhaps he could develop some self-identity through his son's achievement."

Carder goes on to say that Isaac willfully violated God's plan, acting out his own issues upon his son. Isaac and his wife competed for their sons' admiration and approval. Rebekah showered her favoritism upon Jacob; Jacob gave his to Esau.

Favoritism is only one way enmeshment evaporates healthy boundaries. It gets acted out in many other ways in a family. As I briefly mentioned in the previous list, enmeshment, or excessive attachment, can happen when a family is too involved in each other's business. It can happen when a father needs a son to become an all-star to make up for his shortcomings in sports. It can happen when a mother needs her children to remain needy so that she can extend her role as a nurturing mom. It can happen when parents demand that their children be perfect or emulate their parents' behaviors. All of these patterns serve to create an overly dependent person as opposed to the interdependent individual that is the hallmark of a healthy family.

Family Rules

Another marker of a healthy family is that rules are flexible and human, and they assist in creating healthy boundaries. The rules are made for the family and are appropriate for the individuals that live in the family. A critical look at such rules says a great deal about a particular family. Wegscheider-Cruse helps us look at the unrealistic and limiting rules by which many families operate:

- Be nice to everyone.

- Always look on the bright side.

- Control your feelings.

- Don't say anything if you can't say something nice.[4]

These rules make sense on the surface, but closer scrutiny reveals that they are capable of stifling individuality. These rules are impossible to keep and fill people with shame. They foster manipulation and deception. If they are rigidly adhered to, the family will create a brood of robots instead of creative, caring individuals.

What is a better alternative, you ask? Wegscheider-Cruse suggests creating rules that have an honest, reasonable ring to them. She suggests rules such as these:

- You may not hit anyone in the family.
- You are expected to leave the bathtub clean for the next person who will use it.
- You are expected to be home by midnight or call.
- You are expected to treat every person in this family with respect.[5]

Rules within the family that foster individuality are also flexible. As parents, you know that each of your children is different. Each needs different styles of discipline, different forms of love and support, different limits and boundaries. Healthy families allow for individual differences.

I remember the stern scolding I received from my youngest son several years ago. He took me aside and reminded me that he was not his older brother. Just because I needed to set certain limits on his brother, these same limits were not, in his estimation, needed for him. He rightly pointed out that the rules I was imposing were outdated and did not fit him or his circumstances.

My first reaction to his request was to fall back into my old established patterns of parenting. After all, the old rules had worked in raising his brother. Why abandon those tried-and-true techniques? Simply staying the course would have been far easier. Doing so takes less work because we can follow the same recipe that worked before without having to devise an entirely new way of doing things. But that is rarely the best way to provide an environment for creativity and individuality. And *that* is what we are after.

I am a strong supporter of Jim Fay and Foster Cline's program, *Parenting with Love and Logic*. Their approach strives to enlist children in solving their own problems. Fay and Cline see every difficulty as an opportunity for children to enhance their problem-solving skills. Rarely do *Love and Logic* parents use cookie-cutter rules to handle tough situations. Rather, they look at the child with their puzzled, Columbo-like expression, and ask, "How are you going to handle this problem? It sure looks like a tough one to me."

A Family with Boundaries

Making a marriage work is tough stuff. Keeping in touch with your own preferences in a marriage is ongoing work. Add to that the challenge of developing an appropriate interdependence in a family of four, five, or six people. Then add to that mixture children with distinct personalities, needs, and demands. Family life can become incredibly complex.

Let's review God's plan for us and for our families. To do that, we will need to look at the models in Scripture that offer guidance for the development of healthy families. Drawing heavily upon Drs. Townsend and Cloud's momentous work on boundaries, and from their book titled *Boundaries*, we realize that limitations are part of God's design. God designed the universe in an orderly manner. He set boundaries for the seas, the skies, the stars, and the planets. Looking into the great expanse at night or seeing the same patterns day after day gives us a glimpse into the heart of God and His creative order.

In a similar fashion, God designed the family. His plan included parents, or parental figures, to function as leaders. We see this model throughout Scripture: parents leading a family, often including children that are dependent until they reach the stage of autonomy. We also see in Scripture, and in our own experiences, families of differing makes and models. Some have two parents, some have one. Some have several children, some have one or none. But all share similar traits. They all have the need to encourage individuality as well as interdependence on one another. The family must create a safe place to experiment with different roles and behaviors while providing opportunities to develop self-esteem in the process. As we have said, each member is necessary and significant.

Townsend and Cloud help us understand the concept of boundaries within the family. They emphasize that we need lines that indicate where you begin and I end. A line of demarcation that suggests that we are separate. You are not responsible for me or my actions, nor am I responsible for you or your actions. We may be tempted to take care of one another to an excessive degree, but as we have seen before, Galatians 6:2-6 teaches that we are responsible for carrying our own load—that which we are able to carry—and that we are to assist others with the burdens that they cannot carry themselves. Knowing the difference and acting appropriately takes wisdom and insight. The healthy family says, "I will help you when that is appropriate; I will also let you solve your own problems and manage your own life when you can."

The Possibilities of Family

The family is a hallowed institution. Like the church, it is a sacred and safe place to be with God and loved ones. With our family, we can rest, exchange ideas, and take delight in how we have been created.

Mike was a wiry 12-year-old. He came into my office with his ball cap turned backward and jeans slung low off his hips, ready to challenge any authority. His parents had told me that he was beginning to test the boundaries of his family, school, and his own values. His older brother had already entered and exited these testy years. His younger sister was still innocent and asked, "Why does Mike have to be such a jerk?"

They came to my office as a family. Times were rough financially, creating additional instability in their home. But Mike's parents had come to see me years earlier about issues arising with his older brother, and now they were determined to get help for Mike.

Fortunately for Mike, his parents, Jane and Randy, had some experience in dealing with adolescent behavior. They were able to keep things in perspective. Although Mike was angry, they knew that this time of questioning was part of the process of becoming an individual. Drs. Hemfeldt and Warren call this time

> autonomy with attachment...Such a time does not come easily for either parent or child. The process of growth is something like a teeter-totter. One end is dependence, the other is independence. A healthy child learns to stand approximately in the middle and balance the seesaw flat across, one foot on either side of the line.[6]

The task of every person is to find that balance between excessive dependence and desperate independence. Adolescence can be an awkward time of wild flailing from one extreme to another. Even adults struggle to appropriately lean on others while also managing those aspects of their lives that are their responsibility.

I worked with Jane and Randy to find a way to listen to Mike's cries for understanding. We worked together to create an environment where Mike could find his own unique niche in this family. Expecting him to be just like his brother or his sister would be unreasonable. His parents needed to listen carefully to Mike's heart and his yearnings, and to foster his unique development.

Several months later, with a combination of family and individual counseling, the family was much happier. Mike was able to obtain some of the autonomy he was seeking. Randy and Jane granted him a later curfew as he became more responsible with his grades and chores around the house. He was better able to express his differences with his parents and found ways to negotiate more independence. Some of his choices were hard for his parents to accept, but none violated their basic Christian principles and values. The family stretched, with some moaning and groaning, but they have emerged stronger than before.

This family was unique in some ways but very typical in others. They struggled to find a way to provide an opportunity for each member of the family to develop individuality within a larger system of values and expected behaviors. Jane and Randy were able to be flexible while still adhering to certain principles. They were able to negotiate and allow their son to find some of his own solutions. All of this happened in the safe confines of the family. That is precisely what all of us should be aiming for.

How's Your Family?

Families are complex entities. This fact was brought home to me when I asked several people how their families functioned during their childhood years. Specifically, I asked about family meals, as these seem to be where the emotional life of a family is particularly played out. Or, conversely, where it is absent.

One friend shared the following story. Her family, like mine, was required to meet for dinner every evening. However, this was not a happy occasion for the children. They came to dread their "drill sergeant" father who demanded that each child drink a full glass of milk, try at least a bite of everything on the table, and finish everything on their plates. That some of the children were allergic to milk or were too full to finish their meals did not matter; he needed complete control, and he almost got it. However, children find ways to thwart the unrealistic demands of parents. My friend and her siblings discovered all kinds of ingenious ways to avoid finishing their meals. Sadly, the scars of those family encounters, where the promise of real intimacy was never fulfilled, are still with her.

As you read this chapter, were you able to reflect upon the communication patterns in your family? Were you able to consider whether or not the rules are flexible and meet the needs of each child? And what about the issue of autonomy and expression? Do you tolerate different opinions, hairstyles, and dress? More importantly, do you *encourage* such expression? These are just a few of the questions worth considering as you raise your family and make peace with your own childhood.

I remember a helpful explanation of Proverbs 22:6, the famous passage about childrearing. "Train a child in the way he should go, and when he is old he will not turn from it." This passage is usually thought to mean that we are to train children in the ways of the Lord, so that when older they will not leave them. But this particular teacher suggested that the passage tells us that we are to train children according to their natural inclinations rather than forcing them to become something they were never meant to be. Are you encouraging your children to develop their natural gifts and abilities?

The Blessings of Family

This book may find you in a difficult place with your family of origin or your current family. You may be experiencing intense conflict. Some of that conflict may be related to issues discussed in this book, such as establishing and honoring boundaries. You may be wrestling with how others expect you to behave, when you know in your heart that to adhere to other people's expectations would be to violate your own integrity. Your task, as you now know, is to create a safe environment in which you can grow so that you can appropriately meet the needs of others in your family.

As you engage in the lifelong work of understanding yourself and your family, remember that perfect families do not exist. When tempted to grouse about your mother, father, sister, brother, son, or daughter, remember that your family is also a wonderful place for you to practice the skills necessary to navigate life successfully. Think of your family as a setting for practicing the boundary tools you are learning. Consider it a place where people know you and love you but also need to be reminded that you are unique. You have different likes, dislikes, and needs. Practice telling others how you are different, and delight in that difference.

Finally, consider the possibility that belonging to your particular family was no mistake. It was a blessing, hand delivered to you. In times of stress and frustration, you may have told yourself that someone obviously made a terrible mistake at the hospital. In your imagination, you were grabbed by a diabolical set of parents and have suffered needlessly, knowing that your perfect parents are out there somewhere grieving the loss of their innocent child. But carefully consider this: You are right where you are supposed to be. The challenges you are having with your parents, husband, children, and the neighbors are all perfectly designed for your growth. You have the tools to create a wonderful, healthy family because you understand the fine balance between individuality and interdependence. The possibilities are endless.

Reflection

Think about your family of origin.

- Did your family members communicate freely and openly?
- Were your family's rules flexible?
- Were your family members free to fit into different roles on different occasions?
- Did your family value each person?
- Were your family members connected to one another?

Now reflect upon the family you have created as an adult. How is it different from your family as a child? How is it the same? Consider how you can make it the kind of environment where each person is treasured for his or her unique gifts and special contribution.

Chapter Seven

Getting Lost in Friendships and the Workplace

Care about people's approval and you will be their prisoner.

TAO TE CHING

Susan hardly heard the ring of the phone over the cries of her children. "Quiet down!" she yelled as she ran into the bedroom to pick up the receiver, hoping she might be able to hear better there. "Hello," she said impatiently, still frustrated with the girls' behavior. They were four and six and seemed to fight continuously.

"Susan," the voice answered tensely, "it's Jenny. I need to talk. Are you going to be home for a while?"

Without hesitating, Susan told Jenny to come right over. She sensed the urgency in Jenny's voice and immediately offered her friendship. However, after she hung up, she wished that she had not extended the invitation. She was tired and needed to prepare dinner. Her husband, Gary, would be home soon and would expect the family to eat dinner together.

Jenny was a single mother who lived down the street. She and Susan had met at the Mothers of Preschoolers program at church. Jenny had attached herself to Susan immediately. She saw Susan as a woman willing to extend herself for her and took advantage of her generosity. Jenny called at any time, regardless of Susan's family responsibility, asking for help. Though the two were almost the same age, Susan felt a bit of a maternal attachment to Jenny.

A few minutes after hanging up the phone, Jenny knocked at the door. Susan asked the girls to go to the family room. When Susan opened the door, Jenny was standing on the porch, tears streaming down her face.

"What's wrong, Jenny?" Susan asked. "Come in and sit down."

Jenny proceeded to tell Susan about her latest relationship problems. They were the same ones Susan had heard before. Jenny seemed to be in a continual crisis in her relationships. She had been married and divorced twice and was now involved with an alcoholic who was verbally and physically abusive. That afternoon, Jenny's boyfriend had come home drunk, and they had an intense quarrel. When he left, he vowed not to return. In the past this had always meant that he would be back shortly, angrier than ever.

As Jenny poured out her latest saga, Susan found herself wondering when Gary would pull into the driveway. She was also listening for sounds of trouble from the family room. She felt guilty for not paying more attention to Jenny, but she also felt annoyed. Annoyed that Jenny kept placing herself in troubled relationships, annoyed that her daughters could not seem to play without fighting, annoyed that she still had to make dinner and then make lunches for tomorrow. Before she went to sleep she would also have to iron her clothes for work.

As Jenny told of her boyfriend's latest act of stupidity, Susan heard the distinctive rumble of Gary's pickup as he pulled into the driveway. As she struggled with how to tell Jenny that they would have to end their conversation so that Susan could get dinner started, Jenny dropped an unexpected bombshell.

"Would it be all right if I spend the night here?" Jenny said. "I'm afraid of what Bob might do if he comes back tonight."

Just then, Gary walked in the front door.

"Hello, Hon," he said. "Hello, Jenny. How are you doing?" "You don't want to know," she said. "Bob is at it again. I hate to do this to you guys, but I need a place to stay tonight. I wouldn't ask it if it weren't absolutely necessary."

"Stay the night?" Gary looked at Susan. Neither wanted to add this to their list of responsibilities. Yet Susan sensed that Jenny's request was genuine. She really was in turmoil, and her home was unsafe. Jenny desperately needed a helping hand.

What should a friend do now?

Stretched by Friendship

Gary and Susan had discussed this issue before. They had talked about how to set boundaries on friends who asked too much. They had talked about reasonable expectations for friendships.

Friendships rarely fit neatly into clear, well-defined guidelines. You are apt to receive mixed counsel on how best to interact with a friend who does things that make you uncomfortable. We have discussed previously the importance of lending a hand to our neighbors by bearing one another's burdens. But, as Galatians 6:1-5 indicates, we are to offer help to those who cannot help themselves. We are not to bear other people's burdens that they are capable of, and responsible for, carrying themselves. Many people struggle with the blurry line between friendship and personal responsibility.

In attempting to assist Jenny, Susan was stretched beyond her comfort level. Her inner turmoil is a clear signal that Jenny is pushing her boundaries. She genuinely cares about her friend and has developed a loyalty to her. But she also has a strong loyalty to her family and to her own needs. She has a divided heart.

This dilemma has no easy answers. We can see that if Susan gives in to Jenny, she could harm herself and her family. They are waiting for dinner. The girls need attention and supervision. Gary has come home expecting to spend quality time with his family.

Furthermore, Jenny may or may not need to be "rescued" from her plight—she may need to deal with her problem head-on so that it does not recur. As discussed earlier in this book, we should not enable folks when they are struggling with an issue that they need to resolve for themselves.

A Repeated Pattern

Susan's problems with setting boundaries are not limited to Jenny. She has been struggling for some time to find a way to avoid being stretched uncomfortably by her friends. She and Gary have had difficult conversations about the fact that her first commitment is to her husband and family, not to her friends and outside obligations. She has at times, according to Gary, spent too much time and energy serving on committees—to the exclusion of their family.

The issue is not a simple one for Susan. Because she is a likeable woman with boundless energy, she has many friends. She enjoys people and people enjoy her. She has a dynamic personality that attracts others to her. Perhaps her most notable trait is her *helpfulness*. She sees problems and is ready to offer help. She hates to hear about people who are struggling. If her efforts to help others didn't leave her exhausted, we might applaud her willingness to become involved.

Susan's difficulty in balancing commitments is not limited to her involvement with her friends. Susan is a wonderful singer. She leads the soprano section of the choir and is called on often to sing solos. Her talent is a source of pride for her and gives her great joy. On any given day you can find her listening to one of the choir's rehearsal tapes, tirelessly studying her part.

Her gift, however, has a dark side that recently created a challenge for her. The choir director, Caroline, is typically unprepared for Sunday morning services, and Susan often picks up the pieces for her. Caroline is a friend, and Susan hates the choir to sound bad. So when she senses that Caroline needs help preparing the choir, Susan spends extra time with some of the members so that they will know their parts. She cannot resist taking on some of the responsibility even though she knows her friend is being paid to do the job.

What is the problem with what Susan is doing with the choir? What is the problem with her willingness to help Jenny? At first glance, nothing. But at the end of the day, when sitting alone with her husband, she finds herself complaining about having to constantly come to other people's rescue. She wonders aloud why Jenny keeps picking alcoholic men. She wonders why Caroline doesn't prepare properly for their Sunday services. She wonders why everyone relies on her to pick up the pieces. Gary knows the answer. *Because they can!* People will rely on us to the extent that we allow them to do so.

The Effect on the Family

As Gary watches this drama unfold, he too feels annoyed. He sees Susan expend her energy picking up the pieces for others. He watches her energy fade as she drags herself into bed at night. He watches her become short-tempered with their children. He hears of her growing impatience with coworkers. Over the past few years, she has gradually become more irritable. Instead of the bright, bubbly woman he once knew greeting him at the door, he too often finds a stressed-out, frustrated stranger who snaps at him for no reason. Susan is helping others so much that her involvement is hurting her, Gary, and their family.

Gary has challenged Susan to rein in her commitments to others, but so far she has refused to change. She seems intent on protecting, caring for, and generally enabling her friends, all the while complaining of her exhaustion. She and Gary disagree about her situation, and he refuses to listen to her complaints any longer.

I love my wife. She is the friendliest person I know. She will help anyone. Maybe I'm selfish, but I want my wife to have some energy left for the kids and me. I watch her become completely drained by helping other people with things they should be doing for themselves. I watch her spend herself on people who truly are needy, but that doesn't excuse the fact that she is draining herself and has little left over for herself and her family. I could give you a hundred examples of ways she helps out needy people. And at the end of it all she is cranky and tired.

As a result of Susan being cranky and tired, Gary is cranky and tired as well. Susan's lack of boundaries affects her entire family.

Let's look at another example of a codependent friendship, this time between two men.

Longtime Friends

Jesse and Tim had been friends for over 20 years. They had gone to high school together. They loved to laugh about the days when Jesse was a running back for the football team, picking up big yardage behind Tim, a powerful lineman who cleared the way. Tim was the giant while Jesse was the short, slender one. Both had made a mark on the football and baseball teams and had plenty of stories to tell of their glory days.

Their days on the high school sports squads had solidified a friendship that was moving into its third decade. Now both married with children, they had a friendship that had remained, albeit with some lingering problems. As the years passed, tensions that had smoldered began to simmer to the surface.

Tim and Jesse had continued to enjoy some activities together. They both entered the business world, Jesse as an insurance adjuster and Tim as an accountant for a retail firm, and they attended Rotary meetings together. They also routinely got together every fall to go hunting for several weekends. They had bowled on the same team for the last ten years. Jesse enjoyed their friendship at times. At other times, some issues created tension.

Tim raved about their friendship, but Jesse quietly wondered if it was worth maintaining. He was not nearly as comfortable being around Tim as Tim was being around him. Why? Let's listen in on a conversation Jesse had with his wife, Deanne.

"Why don't you want Tim to come over?" Deanne said. "I thought he was your best friend."

"Well, you'd think we were best friends if you heard Tim talk about it. But he's two-faced. He says wonderful things to my face, but then I hear that he's bad-mouthing me behind my back. He's not afraid to borrow things of mine, but when I ask to borrow something from him, it's another story. It's all about Tim. I don't feel like he really cares about me.

"Remember last week?" Jesse continued. "He called me up to see if I could help their daughter move. But what happened two months ago when I asked him to help us install that garage door? He was busy with something else, which is always the case."

"So have you told him how you feel?"

"I've tried, but he turns things back on me. He says that I'm making things up. He denies talking behind my back. He says that I'm just jealous of his success and that I've always been envious of him. Actually, that's probably partly true. But that's not the problem. He won't take any responsibility for his actions. So what choice do I have but to back away?"

"I hate to see you give up a friendship that has lasted for all these years," Deanne said. "I know you guys have a ball together. Can't you just let things go?"

"I've let things go for years. I can't let them go any longer. I just don't want to see him for a while."

Has Jesse done everything he can do to deal effectively with the problem? That is not clear. Should his wife insist that he let the little annoyances go? Probably not. Jesse is no longer comfortable doing that.

As we look closer, we see symptoms of a friendship that is doomed to failure unless both men make some changes. From Jesse's perspective, he feels like he gives more than he gets in return. He feels as if Tim uses him and takes him for granted. When Jesse asks for the reciprocal qualities expected in a friendship, Tim does not offer them. Tim is apparently betraying Jesse's confidence. Jesse's resentment has gradually grown, and he can take it no longer.

In this example of male friendship we can see that Jesse spent years pleasing Tim when it was hurting him. He went along with things when he did not really want to. He buried his hurt and frustration, and now, years later, the friendship is in jeopardy. This is yet another way that excessively pleasing others can take a toll later on.

Codependent Friendships

Codependent friendships are very different from healthy friendships. However, the lines between a healthy friendship and a codependent one can sometimes be blurry. Perfect friendships do not exist. In fact, every friendship has some codependent qualities to it. As you move through this book, you will notice some things that you can change to make your friendships healthier.

As you reflect on the stories presented in this chapter, perhaps you see some patterns. Codependent friendships have unique qualities to them, and you can become an expert at noticing them. This will enable you to eliminate these tendencies from your life, creating healthier and more dynamic friendships. When you are responding to others in a healthier way, your relationships will be healthier, and you will be better equipped to truly help others.

What, then, are the hallmarks of the codependent friendship?

First, *codependent friendships lack healthy boundaries.* A close look at the friendships above illustrates one or both parties making compromises that they do not really want to make. They give up time that they cannot afford to give up. They give of their possessions when they do not want to give them. They really want to say no but cannot seem to do so. In many small ways that build upon each other, they violate their own boundaries.

We have seen that fuzzy boundaries can lead to *enmeshment.* One person is overly involved in the details of another's life. It can involve caretaking, wanting to know more than is needed or helpful, or trying to use another to make ourselves feel better.

Second, *this lack of boundaries creates resentment.* This seems to be a universal phenomenon. When we act against our best intentions, we do not feel good about it. When we give out of our lack, rather than out of our abundance, we feel tired and irritated. We are annoyed and blame others for our bad feelings.

When I hear individuals complain about someone else, I always listen closely to see if they really are the victims or, as is most often the case, if they have betrayed themselves in some fashion. When Susan sits and listens to Jenny while her family waits, she is not being victimized. She is giving away her time freely, albeit with guilt and resentment.

Third, *codependent friendships often occur when we connect with people who have any number of troublesome traits.* Let me list just a few:

- They have problems with addictions to drugs or alcohol.

- They are self-centered, with little respect for your boundaries.

- They are unhappy—unable to create a healthy, happy life of their own.

- They are excessively needy and overly dependent.

- They are ungrateful. Regardless of how much you do, it is never enough.

- They are resentful and blame their problems on others.
- They have trouble with authority.
- They are controlling.

A modern-day proverb asserts, "You are only as good as the company you keep." A variation of this is, "You can only be as healthy as the company you keep."

Fourth, *codependent friendships create a situation where one or both people are trying too hard to please the other.* Sometimes one person is excessively responsible while the other is irresponsible. In other relationships, both people work overtime to please each other. This creates a sticky friendship where one or both are not taking responsibility for their own lives. Neither person is growing into his or her capabilities.

Fifth, *codependent friendships often feed upon problems.* When you stand back and look at codependent friendships, you will see that they lack vibrancy and joy. The relationship feeds upon problems. When some people experience too much joy, they will come up with a big problem to snuff it out. Happiness is a threat to people who thrive on problems.

Sixth, *codependent relationships often have a rescuer and victim.* Someone always needs extra help and attention, and someone is always willing to come to the rescue.

At the beginning of this book I talked about some of the traits of codependency. One of the primary hallmarks of codependency is caretaking. *Codependents make themselves indispensable.* Anne Wilson Schaef, in her book *Co-Dependence: Misunderstood–Mistreated,* notes:

> Codependents really doubt that anyone would want to have them around for their intrinsic worth, so they have to make themselves indispensable. One way of doing this is by "taking care of"—doing things for others they really can and need to do for themselves.[1]

Jockeying for Position

Imagine the scene. We have a tough bunch of young men, boys really, their testosterone raging, who were traveling with the most powerful man on earth. They had no idea of the full extent of His power, but they knew they were part of history in the making. Pretty heady stuff. One can hardly blame them for letting a taste of that power go to their heads. Jesus had the power and influence to turn heads. I suspect the disciples had more than a little swagger in their walk at times.

This kind of power and influence can be fertile ground for many aspects of codependency, as was the case for Jesus and his band of rough and tumble friends. We don't know exactly what happened with this close-knit group, but my guess is that it had many of the dynamics we would find in any other group of friends: posturing for power, sulking when things didn't go their way, gossiping, trying to impress the one in charge. Codependency takes many forms. It existed in people Jesus ministered to. As we peer into the lives of His disciples, we see a certain level of dysfunction.

One glimpse into the immature and manipulative thinking of His disciples is given to us in Mark 10:35-45. James and John went to Jesus secretly, without the other disciples' awareness, and made an absurd request for a privileged position above the rest.

> Teacher, they said, we want you to do for us whatever we ask.
>
> What do you want me to do for you? He asked.
>
> They replied, Let one of us sit at your right and the other at your left in your glory.

We learn that when the others heard of their request for positions of superiority, they were indignant. Jesus had to sit them all down and give them a lesson in servitude. Sounds a little like children in families or employees with their boss, don't you think?

What is dysfunctional about this event? Several things. We see the two brothers going to Jesus secretly. They knew they were doing something wrong. They tried to manipulate their way into a privileged position in order to gain favor. They wanted to use their close friendship with Jesus to gain extra privileges that set them above the rest of the group. Their scheme was brought to light, and they were appropriately scolded by their peers and by Jesus.

Effects of Codependent Friendships

I suspect that as you read this book and learn about some of the traits of the codependent friendship, you are finding traits that apply to yourself. You may also decide that everyone you know is codependent. To some extent that's true. But let's look closer at the result of having codependent friendships.

Perhaps the most important thing to say about codependent friendships is that *they are dysfunctional*. Simply put, they do not function in a healthy way. A dysfunctional car still runs, a dysfunctional job still pays the bills, and a dysfunctional friendship still offers some positive things. But the cost of our involvement is greater than we think. Many of us don't want to look closely at the cost. We would rather deny that a problem exists than face the frightening changes that produce solutions.

Let's look back on Susan's life. Her friendship with Jenny is dysfunctional. Her husband can see, perhaps better than Susan herself, that to always be available as the hero to Jenny's problems does not do anything beneficial for Jenny. Nor does it provide satisfaction for Susan. Everyone loses.

Another effect of the dysfunctional, codependent friendship is that *it will not function effectively or indefinitely*. At some point, the system breaks down. We can see that Jenny's excessive neediness was beginning to wear on Susan. It was beginning to wear on Gary. The wear and tear taking place on their marriage would take a toll at some point because the dysfunctional system will always break down eventually.

Another effect of the codependent friendship is that *it does not encourage people to grow*. Rather than each member of the system becoming stronger and healthier, self-esteem drains away. The rescuers never truly feel better, the heroes never truly feel as if they have won the day, the martyrs never truly feel proud of their situation, the victims always feel worse for being stuck in their plight, the compromisers always feel badly about violating their own boundaries. Rather than a healthy system that encourages and reinforces growth, the dysfunctional, codependent friendship is a downward spiral, doomed to frustration and depression.

Finally, *the codependent friendship does not encourage people to deal with feelings in an effective way*. Such friendships include a lot of denial. The friends tend to mask their feelings, express them in passive-aggressive ways, or deny that they have feelings in the first place. In this type of friendship, feelings are distorted, frozen, held onto, or avoided as something dangerous. This process does not encourage people to express their feelings in a healthy way directly to one another.

Most people that come to my office for counseling have a problem of some sort with codependency. Often this involves relationships with friends and coworkers. When our primary relationships are not going well, we cannot do well.

Most clients can review their lives and note several underlying themes, often hidden, that stem from codependent friendships:

- feeling abandoned—needing to perform to get attention
- feeling hurt and lost—having to do more to gain acceptance
- feeling unappreciated
- feeling undeserving of happiness in a relationship
- feeling undeserving of love

Unfortunately, changing these beliefs and patterns can be difficult. Drs. Hemfelt, Minirth, and Meier, authors of *Love Is a Choice*, note:

> Painful relationships and events that happen early in life become self-repeating and self-fulfilling prophecies. This radar is similar to a tracking system on a commercial aircraft—it sends out a signal and receives a signal. Codependents attract people and are attracted to people who fit the same negative codependent patterns.[2]

The Codependent Workplace

We should not be surprised that those who have trouble setting healthy boundaries in their personal lives also struggle in their work lives. After all, the workplace is made up of numerous relationships with people. Any gathering of people will include challenges. Consider some of the dynamics that make for difficulties at work. People will...

- bring their problems to work
- meddle in others' business
- be unable to communicate effectively
- gossip about others
- act out their frustrations in a passive-aggressive manner
- act immaturely
- be demanding and self-centered

Given these dynamics, we may wonder that any business can function effectively. Actually, businesses sometimes implode emotionally because of the human factor.

Karen came to see me primarily because of problems on the job. She told me that she had been excited to take the job as a teller at a local bank. It was an entry-level job, but she had always wanted to work in a financial institution. She was told that she could expect promotions, the work environment was bright and cheery, and the other employees seemed to enjoy coming to work.

The first couple of months went well. Karen was trained for the job and enjoyed interacting with her customers. She came to know many on a first-name basis. She received a raise after 90 days and felt satisfied with the pay and benefits. Slowly, however, she became disgruntled with other aspects of the job.

"What bothered you about the job?" I asked.

"I'm really starting to dislike some of the other employees. I've always been liked where I work, but here, some of the others seem to have it out for me."

"What makes you say that, Karen?"

"Well, I know how to do my job. But every day one of the women makes a snide comment about how I do things. She can't seem to let a day go by without correcting me. Actually, it's two of the main women. And it's the way they do it. It's not kind and direct. It's sarcastic, and it makes me so angry."

"So, what have you done about it?"

"I have asked them to please talk to me without sarcasm, but it hasn't done any good. They are so immature. I think they are somehow threatened by me, but no one will tell me that to my face. If it doesn't stop soon I'm going to have to quit."

"That would be tough. You really wanted to work at a bank like this."

"Yes, but I don't need the constant reminders of what I am doing wrong. And I don't need to be corrected with sarcasm. I don't need the subtle put-downs."

"Are there other aspects of the job getting to you?"

"Yes. Judy, the lead teller, insists on being a micro-manager. Even after I've proved that I know how to do something, she shows me exactly how it is supposed to be done. It's as if she has to have her hand in everything I do."

"And have you talked to her?"

"No. That lady scares me. She was friendly when she hired me, but I have come to see a different side of her. She is one unhappy woman. She never has a good thing to say about my work. If she isn't criticizing me, I know things must be going okay. But I need to work in an environment that is supportive."

"How do the others handle her micro-managing?"

"I know they aren't happy with it. The longer I am here the more negatives I hear about her. After all, we're professionals. She didn't hire us to watch over us all day long."

Karen was certainly in a dilemma. This was a new job for her, and she did not want to quit after only working there for three months. Also, she wondered if she had really done all she could do to change the work atmosphere. We wondered together whether she had been as assertive as she could be with them. Had she set healthy boundaries?

Work as Family

We spend over half of our lives at work, so when work is going well, we often feel content. Conversely, when work is not going well, we often are troubled. While Sigmund Freud was patently wrong in many respects, he was on target when he said that much of our happiness concerns "love and work." Because work is central to our lives, our relationships there need to be going well in order for us to be happy.

In many respects, our job and our coworkers become a second family. We spend a huge amount of time on the job and often create lasting relationships with people there. When we look closely at our work relationships, we see many of the same patterns being played out that exist in our families and our friendships.

Drs. Hemfelt, Minirth, and Meier, in their book *Love Is a Choice*, list some dynamics that exist in many families and which can be part of a work environment as well. They note,

> Psychologists have also come to recognize that there are certain roles or stereotypes that people assume within a family. All families develop them to a certain extent—the hero, the scapegoat, the lost child, the mascot, and the enabler. For people in a dysfunctional family, these roles become a coping mechanism, a way to get through life with a minimum of upset. They become rigid, mindless patterns of behavior easily visible to those outside the family, yet unrecognized by those within.[3]

Let's briefly look at these five coping strategies, which are essentially ways to limit the pain of living in a dysfunctional, codependent family or work setting.

The Hero. Nearly every work setting has a hero. You know the type who always does things right and is seen as the perfect worker by the boss. The hero rarely causes any problems, always gives 110 percent, and is often a perfectionist.

The Scapegoat. In almost every family or workplace, one person often gets the blame. Whether this individual is truly guilty or not, he or she invariably bears the brunt of things. Sometimes the designated scapegoat agrees to act out the part. Thus, the scapegoat receives negative attention for rebellious behavior.

The Mascot. The mascot earns attention by seizing it. Sometimes described as the clown, the mascot often dilutes the negativity in the group by making jokes. His or her job is to distract everyone from the distressing issues.

The Lost Child. Sadly, these individuals usually go unnoticed. They prefer to be alone and escape the pain of the group by occupying themselves elsewhere. In the work setting, they can be found hunkered down in their cubicle, avoiding the conflict around them. Of course, while they avoid the pain, they also miss out on the pleasure of the group's successes and interactions.

The Enabler. Drs. Hemfelt, Minirth, and Meier note that the enabler's role is played out in each of these other roles. They indicate that the enabler "is a deeper layer behind each of the roles."[4] The enabler may function as a

- placater—always trying to make things better in the family
- martyr—doing anything to make things work out in the family
- rescuer—always trying to solve the family's problems
- persecutor—always fixing the blame on someone
- victim—caught up in self-pity, feeling as though he or she could never be happy

As you reflect on these five roles and the different forms of enabling, try to determine if you have gotten stuck in any of them. Have you fallen into a pattern of interacting as a way of coping with the pain of your particular situation? If so, keep in mind that you can deal with issues more directly, creating a healthy work environment where you can be happy and grow.

Reflection

Codependency is, after all, a way to avoid pain. The roles that we play and the tactics that we use are usually designed to help us feel better inside. When the disciples asked for the favored position, they were seeking a way to feel important. They were trying to fill up something missing inside with a formalized status.

When Susan exhausted herself by being helpful, she was trying, in her own way, to feel significant. When Tim puffed himself up with his friend Jesse, he was indirectly trying to avoid pain and feel significant. But these efforts always fail to yield the intended results.

What are some ways that you act out those roles in the family, with friends, and perhaps at work?

- the hero
- the scapegoat
- the mascot
- the lost child

Fortunately, we can choose healthier ways to avoid pain and find significance. We must neither assume roles that no longer work for us nor resort to helping others to the point of hurting ourselves. Consider some ways of letting go of those overused roles. In the next chapter, we will explore healthy ways to find significance in relationships with our friends and our associates at work.

Chapter Eight

Creating Healthy Friendships and Workplace Relationships

*Friendship improves happiness and abates misery,
by the doubling of our joy and the dividing of our grief.*

MARCUS TULLIUS CICERO

The snow was falling lightly on that December morning, creating a white blanket over the frozen ground. My windshield was layered with an icy veneer and a soft powder. I would need a scraper to get the windows clear enough for driving. A light breeze had dropped the chill factor to nearly 20 degrees, cold by Washington standards.

I had second thoughts about leaving home, and I seriously considered pulling the covers over my head and letting the morning ease under my skin naturally. I would not be seeing clients that day, and the temptation to tuck back into the safety and warmth of my home was overwhelming.

I looked up at the heavy gray clouds and knew that more snow would be coming. My ambivalence grew with every vapory breath. Given the option of staying inside, either in bed or nestled next to a warm fire, or going out to rendezvous with friends, was a tough choice. I steeled myself and decided to brave the weather and the icy roads. My destination that early morning was a collection of men of different backgrounds, ethnicity, and status. We were an unlikely group. Only need could have compelled us to gather when so many other things demanded our attention.

These men are friends, but they are also much more. When women speak of a "circle of friends," I imagine something far more than just people getting together to laugh and cry. I imagine a joining of spirits, a trust that emerges when souls unite. This is what I have with these men. For them I will leave behind my down-filled comforter and blazing fire. I am not obligated to meet with these men. I want to be with them.

What have we created in this sparse room in a simple church building? We have no couch, no fireplace to create ambiance. Only a few chairs and a desk. The lighting is poor and the windows are bare. What fills the room are not things but the Spirit of God and men. Together we have been graced to create something that is wonderful.

When we formed the group, we knew that we were trying something that would likely fail. Think about it. A group of men determined to meet and confidentially share their needs? Ridiculous. Men don't do that! We wouldn't last more than eight weeks. But six years later, there we were, ignoring the elements on a chilly winter morning to share each other's company and counsel. Most of the members are the same ones that showed up at our first meeting.

Over the years, we have shared many large and small details of our lives with one another. They know that I took each of my sons fishing in Alaska with my father. They know that I wished I had stayed with piano lessons and that I fear confrontation. I know that two of the men have been unfaithful, and another struggles with alcohol. These are intimacies that draw us together.

As I followed another early-morning traveler's tracks in the snow, I wondered how we could still find value in meeting, some 300 meetings after our initial get-together. What qualities nurtured our group? Perhaps they are the same qualities that keep any friendship together or any group of employees bound to one another. Let's look at what constitutes healthy friendships and what sustains them.

Qualities of a Healthy Friendship

As I think about my group and the ingredients that make it successful, I am confident that these same qualities are what make other relationships successful as well.

Confidentiality

At our first group meeting we made a pact. It was a critical ground rule, a formal agreement that is usually an informal part of other friendships. We would keep one another's confidence. What was said in the group would stay in the group.

We have experienced the healing power of being able to say whatever we want to say and know that it will be kept confidential. That is what I love about this group and what I enjoy about writing in my journal. It is what I find critical in any friendship as well. What I say cannot be misconstrued or used against me. No matter what spills out during the heart murmurings I offer on these Friday mornings, my friends will not gossip about me.

Purpose

Our group formalized our gathering by stating that we were there to offer support. We emphasized that our job was not to chat about how the Blazers did last night or whether the Seahawks would finally make it to the playoffs. Small talk would be saved for another time. This time and place was set apart for sharing our concerns.

Friendships can be arranged this same way. Women's groups often clarify that their friendship is special, perhaps even sacred. They clarify that they gather for a purpose, and they remind each other that sharing their concerns with one another in a confidential and purposeful manner is not to be taken lightly.

Listening

The human psyche may have no deeper need than to be listened to and to be understood. Psychologists use much of the therapeutic hour to listen to their patients. To be listened to is healing. We all long for someone to take an active interest in our lives by asking questions so that we can share our excitement about what is stirring in our souls. Active listening is present not only in my men's group but also in my other friendships. When people listen, we feel that what we are saying is meaningful and that we are important.

The psychological profession takes more than its share of chiding for selling "listening." However, a listening ear is a prized commodity. It is not easily given, nor easily obtained. When Dan Rather interviewed Mother Teresa, he asked her what she said to God when she prayed.

"Nothing," she said. "I just listen."

Not content to leave it at that, Rather asked, "Then what does God say to you?"

"Nothing," she said. "He just listens."

Without Judgment

We need a place where we can empty our mind-maze wonderings without judgment. Each of us needs a place where we can share our fears without being criticized. No one helps us when he or she says, "You don't need to feel that way." Well of course we don't need to, but the point is that we do! We don't need others to shame our way of thinking or our behavior. In most cases, we've already done a pretty thorough job of belittling ourselves. We need a place of acceptance where we can voice our thoughts without the fear of lectures about right and wrong.

You may balk at that. You might be thinking that we need to be told that what we are doing is wrong. I disagree. I suggest that judgments be reserved for those invited to offer feedback. Even if judgment is requested, I think it should be offered sparingly. Jesus' counsel is, "For in the same way you judge others, you will be judged, and with the measure you use, it will be measured to you" (Matthew 7:2).

A Safe Environment

A growth-enhancing friendship offers a place where a person can explore their issues. They are able to think out loud, knowing that their thinking will not be judged. This is an incredibly liberating experience, especially considering how often we may fear judgment, shame, or ridicule. When we find a friendship that feels safe, we have found something very valuable.

This safe environment is a place where we can express our views and try on different aspects of our personality. All of us wonder, at times, what trying something new would be like. "What if I sold the business and went back to art school?" "What if I were to take my son on that outdoor adventure program?" "What if I were to take that writing class I have always been dreaming about?" We may be afraid to actually take action, but we want to "test the waters" of these ideas. This requires a safe environment.

Giving Advice Sparingly

Our group also agreed to offer advice sparingly. This decision resulted from studies of other groups that have found that offering advice is generally detrimental. Offering pat answers for complex problems is far too easy. One or more members of a group or friendship may be tempted to pontificate on a topic. No one wants to hear someone else wax eloquent on the lessons of life.

I must admit that I bristle when I hear talk show therapists offering solutions as if they were penny candy. "Here," they seem to say, "take a little of this, and you will feel better." We grab their platitudes, such as "Move on with your life and don't cry over a broken relationship," and try to make them work. The advice sounds simple enough. But as soon as we hang up the phone or turn off the television, we realize that their advice is like candy all right— cotton candy. It disappears as soon as it hits your tongue. It is not real; it is merely bad advice, given too quickly for the purpose of entertaining, not healing.

Shared Experience

The twelve-step plan of Alcoholics Anonymous says that its members gather "to share our experience, strength, and hope." Not a bad reason to get together. I find that those are good reasons for any friends to gather.

As I drove through the snow on that cold December morning, I was anxious to meet with those who had shared my experiences. Not that each of them had experienced everything I had or vice versa, but by sharing our stories we had shared our personal histories.

We share our story with a limited number of people. Only a few know the agonies you have suffered through or the mountains you have climbed. The unique tapestry that comprises the story of you has been told only a few times. This is the shared experience that has so much power to uphold, protect, and nourish our souls.

Humor

We can endure nearly anything if we have friends to support us and, perhaps just as importantly, if we can find the humor in the situation. As we stand back and gain perspective, humor shared with our friends makes our problems much more tolerable.

Good friends do not take themselves or our daily problems too seriously. They are able to tease us into seeing the lighter side of a situation while allowing us ample room to grieve and feel our losses.

Encouragement, Not Caretaking

As you have been learning in this book, we must perform a balancing act when caring for others. The healthy friend is able to empathize with your struggles but not become overly enmeshed in them. You will not receive any meaningful help from those who become mired down in your difficulties.

When Dr. Jan Yager, author of *When Friendship Hurts*, talks about this issue, she says that the ideal friend has

> clear and appropriate boundaries between "me" and "you"...Respect for feelings, experiences, possessions and relationships helped him [the ideal friend] to develop the ability to be there for his friend, but not to be overly involved in his friends' lives, decisions or other relationships.[1]

Challenging

Ideal and healthy friends know when we need encouragement and when we need some light challenges. They know they cannot tell us what to do and dare not judge our actions, regardless of how immature they may seem at times. But they find ways to measure out challenges for us. They can sense when we are asking to be pushed beyond our comfort zones, but they do not force us to move faster than we are now.

The line between *encouragement* and *challenge* is a blurry one, but I see these terms as warm and engaging, not harsh and distancing. As you consider ways in which you can be a good friend and as you look for safe and healthy friends, you will recognize the difference between being pushy and being encouraging.

Becoming Our Best Selves

Friendships offer us a place to become our best selves. In fact, we have no better place to emerge into the people we are trying to become than in deep, abiding friendships. A renowned researcher on women's development, Carol Gilligan, said, "We know ourselves as separate only insofar as we live in connection with others, and… we experience relationship only insofar as we differentiate other from self."

In her book *Connecting: The Enduring Power of Female Friendship*, Sandy Sheehy discusses the influence of female friendships.

> Intimate friendships with smart women brought Eleanor Roosevelt out of her shell and gave her the savvy and self-confidence to become perhaps the most effective First Lady in history…At first Eleanor was awed by her friends' careers, but soon they helped her recognize her own insight, judgment, and organizational abilities.[2]

We are all engaged in the process of becoming our best selves. Men enjoy relationships, but we are often reluctant to really connect with other men. We do so usually in the context of physical activities such as golf or basketball. This is what makes my men's group so unique. We gather for the sole purpose of knowing and connecting with other men.

Women, on the other hand, seem to relish the notion of connecting. Relationships take a central position in their lives. As Sheehy again notes, "We delight in them, worry about them, nurture them, and focus our creative and intellectual energy on them. Even when they don't involve us, they form a favorite subject for conversation, for books, and for movies."

Although connecting with other women is important, she identifies the dangers I have described in this book. "A friendship that requires that one person alter her experiences or remold her personality to meet the other's needs inhibits and distorts development."[3]

Jonathan and David

Perhaps the most celebrated and poignant friendship in Scripture is that of Jonathan and David. They became best friends amid tragedy. David was enlisted as a general in King Saul's army. After proving his military prowess, David advanced in the ranks. He later married Saul's daughter and became best friends with Saul's oldest son, Jonathan.

In many ways the friendship was an unlikely one. Jonathan was, after all, the son of the king of Israel, who was soon to be David's adversary. Saul perceived David as a threat, and Jonathan was placed in the precarious position of choosing loyalties. The situation had all the makings of a drama involving triangulation.

But as we read of their friendship, we see that David and Jonathan had several qualities necessary for an enduring, healthy friendship. In spite of the fact that Saul handpicked David to be a general in his army, Saul soon realized that David would be a threat to his kingdom. Jonathan chooses to remain loyal to David, just as David had remained loyal to Saul.

Several qualities strengthened the friendship David and Jonathan enjoyed. In 1 Samuel 20, we note that *even in the midst of war and tragedy*, their friendship contained these traits:

- honesty
- loyalty
- emotional support
- selfless love

Jonathan's loyalty to David continued in spite of his father's attempts to kill David. When Jonathan warned David of Saul's intentions, we read of their emotional encounter.

> After the boy had gone, David got up from the south side of the stone and bowed down before Jonathan three times, with his face to the ground. Then they kissed each other and wept together—but David wept the most. Jonathan said to David, "Go in peace, for we have sworn friendship to each other in the name of the LORD" (1 Samuel 20:41-42).

What a wonderful picture we have of deep friendship and brotherly love. You are not likely to see two men act this way today, but we can be inspired by this biblical model of two men who dared to offer friendship and love for one another even when doing so meant that they were risking death.

The Relationally Healthy Company

Friendship is critical in our personal lives, but equally important are healthy relationships in our professional lives. Because we spend so much of our lives at work, and it is the place that potentially offers us confidence and satisfaction, healthy relationships at work are not optional—they are imperative.

In the last chapter, I noted many of the things that can go wrong at work. Some of the pitfalls include poor boundaries, gossip, and stepping on others' feelings for the sake of personal advancement. Let's review what healthy relationships at work look like.

Work relationships are similar to personal friendships, but they are different in several critical ways.

- We go to work to do a job. We are not there to socialize, gain confidentiality, or to bare our souls. We go there to work!

- Work relationships are not meant to become too personal. We may socialize after work, but business ethics and behavioral protocols should prevail.

- We get paid to do a job. While we might not always like the people with whom we work, that does not need to stop us from working for a particular company.

Having said that, let's look at some similarities between personal friendships and workplace relationships. What are some things we can expect from our work, and how can we make it a healthier place to be?

- Firm boundaries should be in place, which means keeping the workplace free from excessive personal information. The office has no room for gossip.

- When we feel that we are not being treated fair on the job, a workplace ethic should allow for the free expression of dissatisfaction. We must have the opportunity to be heard and understood and be free to offer constructive criticism.

- We must feel appreciated, encouraged, and respected for what we bring to the job. We must have room for creative expression. We must feel that we are being fairly compensated.

- We need a free flow of communication. Messages must be straight, clear, and direct.

- We should know exactly what is expected of us. Fuzzy expectations only breed anxiety and cause trouble down the line.

- Companies must promote healthy values. We want to work for a company that genuinely cares for others and does not take unfair advantage of employees.

David Whyte discusses a critical intangible we can strive for at work in his marvelous book, *Crossing the Unknown Sea.*

The severest test of work today is not of our strategies but of our imaginations and identities. For a human being, finding good work and doing good work is one of the ultimate ways of making a break for freedom.[4]

Whyte suggests that we need an opportunity to be wild, to express our creative energies in ways never before attempted.

A Word from Mister Rogers

When I think of goodness, simplicity, honest values, and integrity, my list of examples is very short. We have all come to be disillusioned by those whom we thought were good, only to discover their foibles and be sorely disappointed. Perhaps the message is clear—be careful whom you place on any pedestal.

As we talk about having good boundaries and being good friends, I think this chapter would be incomplete without a bit of sage counsel from Mister Rogers—our guide on the path of neighborliness. Quoting Jesus and Mister Rogers in the same chapter may seem odd, but I believe they share many of the same positive qualities pertaining to relationships. Pull up a chair, pour yourself a cup of tea, and listen to a few quotations from Mister Rogers' book, *The World According to Mister Rogers*.

As human beings, our job is to help people realize how rare and valuable each one of us really is, that each of us has something that no one else has—or ever will have—something inside that is unique to all time. It's our job to encourage each other to discover that uniqueness and to provide ways of developing its expression.

All of us, at some time or other, need help. Whether we're giving or receiving help, each one of us has something valuable to bring to this world. That's one of the things that connect us as neighbors—in our own way, each one of us is a giver and a receiver.

When you combine your own intuition with the sensitivity to other people's feelings and moods, you may be close to the origins of valuable human attributes such as generosity, altruism, compassion, sympathy, and empathy.

As different as we are from one another, as unique as each one of us is, we are much more the same than we are different. That may be the most essential message of all, as we help our children grow toward being caring, compassionate, and charitable adults.[5]

Every day we have the opportunity to be a good neighbor. Look around and see who needs some neighborliness in your world. I suspect you will not have to look far.

Christ & Co.

When we look at Christ's ministry, we see an illustration of a healthy company—as well as much of what Mister Rogers promoted concerning neighborliness and simple friendship. Not only do we see healthy relationship principles at work, but we also see healthy workplace principles as well. This should not surprise us since Christ is our model for healthy relationships.

As we view Christ's unfolding ministry we see several components worth mentioning. Christ shared His vision in a simple, straightforward manner. He didn't demand that anyone follow His teachings. His friendly style, in concert with his convincing message, was contagious. His disciples and many others caught the fire of His mission and decided to join His companionship and "company." Christ shared His mission and purpose clearly, though certainly many did not truly understand. His communication with His disciples (His "employees") was clear, compelling, compassionate, convincing, and consistent. "Come, follow me, and I will make you fishers of men." He never wavered from His direction. At times, His message was disturbing; at times, loving; at times, incredibly compelling. His purpose was powerful, most importantly, because He had what others wanted. He offered the path to eternal life and perfect peace in this life.

There you have principles that would effectively guide any company today. You have the principles that would create relational balance at the workplace. You have the tools to create a healthy, balanced friendship. Christ modeled these traits:

- respect and dignity for His followers
- a shared mission
- clear communication
- an opportunity to be useful and creative
- friendship and companionship

Reflection

Friendship, whether in our personal lives or at work, must contain many different ingredients to be successful. Many relationships are lost in a fog of emotions, and without clear boundaries to give direction, they can be dashed to pieces on the rocks of hurt feelings. Dangers are everywhere. We must know where they lie and be skilled enough to steer clear of them.

As you think about your relationships, do you offer these qualities?

- a place of safety
- a place of wildness
- a place to simply be

- a place to be understood
- a place to test new behaviors and new ideas

I hope that you will be inspired to provide some of these qualities to those who grace your world.

Chapter Nine

Controlling Churches

We must not think the worst of good truths for their being preached by bad ministers; nor good laws for their being enforced by bad magistrates.

MATTHEW HENRY

Everyone knew her as May, though that was not her real name. I didn't realize that for years, but one afternoon the aging woman confided in me that her given name was Leona. She had been named after her mother's sister. She never liked her aunt, and she disliked her name even more. As a young woman, she decided to adopt the name May because of her favorite month of the year. "Spring is such a special time," she said with a twinkle in her eye. "The flowers are starting to bloom, the air is thick with the fragrance of lilacs and daffodils, and the days are getting longer. What can you find wrong with May?"

Her springlike disposition fit May perfectly. She was the secretary of the church where I worked as the janitor while putting myself through graduate school. Regardless of how grouchy I might be, May was always sweet, kind, and generous. The other janitors and I could always count on her to bring cookies to the office and to compliment us about something we had done.

While I busied myself with cleaning the church, May always kept pace. She was the person who kept the church running smoothly. She answered phones, sorted and stacked bulletins, managed the pastor's schedule, and did the myriad other things that go unnoticed. She never demanded much for herself, and she didn't receive much, from what I could see.

I remember being shocked one day when I perused the annual church report and saw how small her salary was. I was paid better, and my responsibilities paled in comparison to hers. I was so surprised by May's meager wages that I asked the pastor if the report was accurate. He assured me that it was and then commented that no one works at a church for the money. I didn't confess my primary motivation for working there.

What bothers me to this day is that the church seemed to condone the situation. Tacitly, the pastor and the church council were content to take advantage of an older woman who could barely make ends meet. They watched as she gave herself, and her time, to the life of the church, almost as though this was what was expected of her.

Many years later, I also gave too much to a church. However, my motives were different from May's. Unlike May, who seemed to give out of compassion and genuine concern, I gave out of pride. And coercion. And control.

Being Used

I didn't really see it coming, though I had been warned to be careful. "You will be used for what you have to offer, and when you are no longer needed, you will be set aside," said one of my friends. "I've seen it happen before. Be careful."

I was puzzled as to why I would need to be cautious. I have grown up in the church and watched my father serve the church selflessly. I never thought he was being used. Like May, he seemed to offer his talents and gifts where needed. He had financial skills, so he served as church treasurer for years. He had the gift of leadership and was elected church chairman more times than I can remember. My father had gifts; the church had needs. But he had a family too, and I must admit that I sometimes felt like the church received the better part of him. Although I never heard him complain, I know that my mother worried about his level of involvement on more than one occasion.

My personal struggle began when I visited a church one Sunday, looking for a place where I could hear the word of God preached. The speaker was eloquent and kept his parishioners spellbound. I knew immediately that this was a place where I could be taught a great deal and grow in my faith. And I did.

As soon as I began regular attendance, Pastor Jay seemed to take a liking to me. We were close to the same age and enjoyed many of the same hobbies and interests. Our friendship grew, and as it did he encouraged me to participate more in the life of the church. I was flattered. He noticed that I had good speaking skills and asked me to join him in a weekly radio broadcast. The program received good reviews, partly because of his oratory skills and partly because of mine. Again, I was flattered.

Before long, Pastor Jay asked how I would feel about teaching a Sunday school class. The church needed an instructor for several classes on family life issues, which is my specialty, so I accepted the offer. The classes were well attended and I received kudos from the church body and from Pastor Jay. My ego grew as I became part of the elite inner circle of the church. Secretly, I could feel my pride being touched and my ego swelling, but I also sensed that something else below the surface was wrong.

I remained very active, the programs I was involved in grew, and my relationship with Pastor Jay became stronger. He confided in me about his plans for the church. He envisioned the church doubling in size and said that I would be an instrumental player in that growth.

Again, I was proud of my church, my relationship with the pastor, and my role in the action.

The church did grow and wonderful things happened. Lives changed. People were excited about the new programs, about the way God was working in the body of our church, and about the future. Yet some people questioned what was taking place. Rumors began to spread that Pastor Jay was an egotist. Some members left the church after being hurt by him. Could the rumors be true, I wondered? Was all of this growth good? What was the cost of our progress? I could see the effect on my own life. I had become busier and busier as I felt compelled to maintain a frenetic pace in my work at the church.

The church continued to grow, and my responsibilities grew with it. Pastor Jay asked me to start a lay counseling program, which I did. He asked me to lead retreats, which I did. He asked me to join the church staff, which I did not do. I wanted to maintain some degree of separation between what I did professionally and what I did for the church.

What bothered me most, however, was that I could sense that something was very wrong. I do not want to cast blame on anyone; what happened to me took place with my permission and full participation. But the same thing happens to too many people, and they are hurt in the process. I participated in a process of destructive collusion. The church offered me a huge amount of ego-stroking and flattery—more than I had ever known before. They offered me an opportunity to be a part of a powerful inner sanctum. They offered me affirmation and acceptance, which all codependent people pleasers need.

One of the most destructive habits of the controlling church is offering acceptance with a price. I was accepted and affirmed only if I attended church services three times a week. Anything less was intolerable. I was accepted if I tithed regularly and if I agreed with the pastor about the content of our broadcast. If I disagreed with Pastor Jay, he scolded me. I knew that to enjoy my favored position I would have to fall in line. I would have to give up being me. And for a season I did. But my doubts began to grow, and I questioned my relationship with the pastor and the church.

My church leadership role ended when I refused to conform to the church's expectations. Were Pastor Jay and the church members wrong in forcing those standards upon me? I believe they were. Ultimately, each of us must make this determination. The line between expectation and obligation is fuzzy. When people are unable to draw a line between them, they get caught up in trying to be something they are not. As a result, they are no longer able to think, feel, or choose for themselves.

Betrayed

May served for years out of dedication and loyalty, but the result for her was not entirely different than it was for me. Years later, she wondered why she got a sinking feeling in the pit of her stomach when she reflected on those years of service to her beloved church. So many other people like her gave selflessly, she thought, only to be disappointed in the end. They gave in the Sunday school classrooms as teachers, they watched over the toddlers and infants in the nursery. They gave in the choir and served on the elder board. They gave and gave and gave. Some felt honored to be of service. But May knew from talking to other church members that something changed somewhere along the way for many of them.

They began to feel used. They began to feel, as did I, that they were no longer wanted and needed. The church only wanted and needed what they could provide. This is the feeling at the heart of the betrayal. Someone you have grown to care deeply about turns on you. You hope for honor in return for loyal service but instead receive criticism for failing to conform. You expect some praise for good performance but receive that nod of the head that says you have merely done what was expected of you. Your heart sinks, and you feel used.

The pain comes when you begin to realize that you compromised your integrity to fit into the machinery of the church. You no longer feel good about yourself or your faith.

Something changes when individuality is lost. Close scrutiny of the situation revealed that the needs and desires that May and I had were no longer considered important. What was important was how we could be molded to fit into the church's master plan.

The process is usually so insidious that most people do not realize it is taking place. Just as one can become lost in a marriage, family, or any organization, one can easily become lost in a church. This may not necessarily translate into a church's blatant disregard for your helpfulness or your gifting. More often, it is a gradual tug that eventually pulls you deeper and deeper into the moving stream. If you are not careful, you will drown.

Denial is something we can recognize. Denial is a form of protection. It shields our egos by refusing to acknowledge or confront what is painful. We may notice our denial, but we rarely wake up and recognize that we are losing our individuality to the goals and rules of the larger organization. Rarely does the leader—in this case, the pastor—consciously recruit people to serve his or her egocentric goals. No, the process is much more subtle than that and usually far less malevolent. Regardless of the pastor's intent, the end result is a feeling of betrayal.

Why might you feel betrayed? Because you realize that you are being used, that your individuality is being consumed. In God's heart, you are valued for who you are and for your gifts that ben efit the body. The Scriptures do not say that your gifts and personality must be altered to fit into the grander schemes of the church.

The Scriptures say that the church benefits from the uniqueness of each believer. The apostle Paul's words are strong:

> God has given each of us the ability to do certain things well. So if God has given you the ability to prophesy, then prophesy whenever you can—as often as your faith is strong enough to receive a message from God. If your gift is serving others, serve them well. If you are a teacher, do a good job of teaching (Romans 12:6-7 TLB).

Notice that this passage does *not* say this:

> Please do whatever you can do to make your gifts fit into the goals of the pastor. If he or she says you are to be a speaker, even though your gift is in prophesying, please start writing sermons. Do not spend any time thinking or praying about developing your particular gifts. That is not what is important. You are to become whatever the body needs. Blend in, give up yourself, and serve.

I offer this absurd argument to make a point. When the leaders of any organization lose sight of the uniqueness of their members, they have made a grave mistake—one that will damage the body of believers and leave its members feeling betrayed.

The church and its leaders did not set out to betray May, my father, or me. But they forgot the fundamentals of good leadership, and we ended up following like trusting sheep. We participated fully in the process, as do many others every day. As you are discovering, you can lose yourself in many ways to many programs and people. Sadly, the church is another place where we try to please others, and in doing so we can end up hurting ourselves.

When we give ourselves completely to someone and they do not meet our expectations for appropriate recognition, we feel betrayed. May felt betrayed when the church did not honor her faithful service after nearly 20 years. When she retired, they gave a small luncheon for her and then left her to struggle on Social Security. She could not help but feel wounded by her beloved church.

I felt deeply betrayed by my church. I gave many hours of service, and when I was no longer effectively meeting the needs of my pastor, he disposed of me. The same thing happened to many others at that church. The pastor used people to move the organization in the direction he intended it to go. Countless others in too many churches have experienced the same thing.

My father has never mentioned feeling betrayed. After 50 years, he and my mother continue to attend the same church. Mom and Dad love that church, as do I. But has the church honored him appropriately for his years of service? Did he give too much of himself at times, hurting himself and his family in the process? These are questions he has grappled with in recent years. I believe he would say today that he gave willingly because he felt called to service. His reward was the understanding that he was making a difference in the kingdom of God. May would say much the same thing. But does that negate the responsibility of the church to properly care for the individual's needs?

Group Think

Some time ago, psychologists coined the term *group think*. It is the tendency of any organized group of people to stifle individuality and encourage conformity. Most of us have been advised to adhere to "the way we do things around here." Since early childhood we have been schooled in the fine art of being civilized, also known as conforming to the expectations of the person in charge—the teacher. Can you remember being in a classroom and feeling petrified to share your opinion on a certain subject? Scared to death to stand out and facing public ridicule, you figured out what the teacher wanted you to say, and you said it.

Most groups experience the same thing. Psychologists use the term *demand characteristics* to describe the expectations groups have for individuals to behave in a prescribed manner. For example, imagine preparing for a dinner party with friends. As you begin to plan for the outing, you consider who will be there. You try to determine the dress code and what people will be bringing. You recall other dinner parties you have attended and mentally prepare a set of behaviors for this one. Most likely you will imagine yourself fitting into the expectations of the group. You will probably not do or say anything outrageous for which you would be criticized.

These demand characteristics are very helpful because they reduce our anxiety and help us understand how to behave. But they also create conformity and stifle individuality. Only a very secure person can venture off the beaten path and say or do things that might raise an eyebrow.

I have a dear friend and professional colleague who sniffs at conventionality. Fred is a financial whiz and worth a bundle, but his hair is rarely combed and his clothes always look tattered. He has numerous cars, each in a state of disrepair. These broken vehicles mirror his appearance, but they do not bother him. He has no desire to take on the stereotypical persona of a highly credentialed professional.

I once rode to a conference with Fred. During the trip, he trimmed his beard while driving. I watched in shock as one hand clutched the wheel while the other operated his trimmer. The whiskers fell on his lap.

"Fred," I said in amazement. "You're going to make a mess of your car, not to mention that you might just kill us both."

"So?" he said smiling. "Nobody rides in it but me, and I don't mind."

At the conference, he spoke up often and loudly, gave the speakers a bad time, and generally disregarded the accepted protocol for such a meeting. While annoying at times, his gusto for following his own path was fascinating. Fred fought tirelessly against the forces of conformity.

Although many people are uncomfortable with people like Fred, we are also often amused by them. Something makes us admire their daring nature. Faced with the pressure to conform, they fight against it. This is something we should all attempt to emulate.

Let's now look more closely at some very destructive characteristics of the controlling church and its impact on the pleasing personality.

Spiritual Abuse

When a person with a pleasing, codependent personality meets someone with a charming, controlling, and dominating personality, trouble is bound to occur. When it happens in a church, spiritual abuse is often the result. Because so little is known or understood about the topic, the whole idea sticks in people's craws. Surely, spirituality and abuse should be mutually exclusive. But sadly, this is not so. Now, more than ever before, we see the results that stem from the misuse of power and authority in the church. When someone has power and authority over others and uses that power to hurt, God's heart is grieved. This was never His intention for leaders of the church, but it is happening in many, many churches.

Ken Blue, in his book *Healing Spiritual Abuse,* says, "Spiritual abuse happens when a leader with spiritual authority uses that authority to coerce, control or exploit a follower, thus causing spiritual wounds." He goes on to say, "Spiritual abuse may differ from some other forms of abuse in that it is rarely perpetrated with the intent to maim." The perpetrators may be "so narcissistic or so focused on some great thing they are doing for God that they don't notice the wounds they are inflicting on their followers."[1]

Blue uses the example of servers in an upscale restaurant. Servers are trained in the vocabulary and body language of friendliness and familiarity, and they use it to gain our trust. They then use that trust to entice us into ordering what the restaurant wants to sell and, of course, to extract as much money as possible while making the customer feel loved and cared for. The church can, at times, treat individuals as if it were selling them a product.

Jeff VanVonderen, another leader in our understanding of spiritual abuse and author of *The Subtle Power of Spiritual Abuse*, states,

> It's possible to become so determined to defend a spiritual place of authority, a doctrine or a way of doing things that you wound and abuse anyone who questions, or disagrees, or doesn't "behave" spiritually the way you want them to. When your words and actions tear down another, or attack or weaken a person's standing as a Christian—to gratify you, your position or beliefs while at the same time weakening or harming another—that is spiritual abuse.[2]

> Among my people are wicked men who lie in wait like men who snare birds...their houses are full of deceit; they have become rich and powerful...Their evil deeds have no limit; they do not plead the cause of the fatherless...they do not defend the rights of the poor (Jeremiah 5:26-28).

A Taboo Emotion

I resisted thinking of myself as a victim of spiritual abuse. I assumed that victims of spiritual abuse would have severe symptoms. Instead of looking more deeply at my wounds, I minimized my hurt. I have come to understand that Christians commonly downplay the extent to which they have been hurt by their pastors or church leaders. To be angry with your pastor feels a bit like being angry with God—a taboo emotion, even though we see the psalmist having more than a few feelings like this. After some time, I saw that my experience was quite similar to that described by Blue.

After reflecting about what happened to me, I see that my charismatic pastor could sell Christianity. He had a great plan for the church that was hard to fault. He wanted church growth and notoriety. He hoped that we would all become known in the community for our programs. Criticizing this plan was very difficult. To oppose or even question it would be to incur his wrath, disapproval, and for the codependent, the loss of his acceptance. The stakes for playing on this turf are high, and I have watched many get hurt and fall by the wayside.

The signs that I might be in for a fall of my own came early in my ministry experience. They came in the form of warnings from friends. "Watch out," they said. "Pastor would like to use your credentials for his own glory. He would like to use what you have to offer and then push you aside."

I am thankful that I was leery enough to heed some of their warnings. I took a fall, but their advice softened the blow. After hearing stories of others who were taken in by his charm and then hurt terribly by his callous dismissals, I was on the alert. As Ken Blue states, such people have their own agenda and are so caught up in it that they are often not aware they are hurting those left in their wake.

Spiritually abusive leaders are like the Pharisees described in the New Testament. The Pharisees exercised authority over the people, sometimes creating an atmosphere of fear and abject obedience. They established a set of rules and regulations to protect the law. Blue says,

> Today, when church leaders set themselves up as keepers of the gate, using religious performance rather than faith in Jesus as the criterion for acceptance or rejection, they become the strategically misplaced leaders who thwart the life of the body of Christ. In so doing they perpetuate the ministry of the Pharisees.[3]

In the Pharisaic community, as in many churches and organizations today, control of people is the central issue. As C.S. Lewis once said, "If the divine call does not make us better, it will make us much worse. Of all bad men, religious bad men are the worst."[4]

We must remind ourselves that certain conditions set the stage for spiritual abuse to occur, and one of them is our presence. An abusive leader has no power to abuse or hurt others unless we grant him or her that power. Patricia Evans, in her book *Controlling People*, is extremely insightful in offering clues to help us avoid these problems in the future. Speaking of individuals who are controlled in relationships, she says:

> Having learned to deny their own wisdom and having taken in other people's definition of them, without even realizing it, those who are disconnected from themselves construct an identity not grounded in experience but constructed out of, or in reaction to, other people's ideas, expectations and values.[5]

I believe that Ms. Evans has hit upon several key issues. Looking closely at them will help us to become stronger and to work cooperatively with our pastors and church leaders for our spiritual growth and the proper worship of God.

- We must learn to identify our own wisdom, grounded in the Word of God. We cannot be spoon-fed dependents, waiting to receive all truth from fallible men and women. God has promised to give us wisdom, in generous doses, if we search for it (Proverbs 2:1-6).

- We dare not take on others' definitions of us. We are not what other people think of us. Our identity is grounded and rooted in God's opinion of us. We are His workmanship, His people, crowned with glory and honor, in charge of creation, holy, and called brothers by God (Hebrews 2:7-11).

- We must guard against becoming disconnected from ourselves. If we do not spend time listening to our heartbeat, to our thoughts and opinions, we will be vulnerable to accepting others' definitions of how things ought to be. We must learn to be connected to ourselves, to our spiritual gifts, and to our ability to discern the spirits.

- Finally, we must look at how we view the world. Is our view simply a regurgitation of what someone else has told us? Or is it a point of view that has been formed out of the crucible of prayer, discernment, reflection, and study?

God's Design for the Church

God certainly did not design the church to be a place where people are hurt and authority is abused. This is not in His heart. Excessive control in the church is a misuse of God's authority. As I share stories of this misuse, and as you recall patterns of spiritual abuse in your life, we can easily rail against it. I could be tempted to become cynical and push away from the formal structure of the church. Like many others, I am tempted to worship the God of creation in the natural world, away from leaders and people who might contaminate the experience. But something beckons me back to the assembly and the call from Scripture that we not abandon meeting together. God knows something about the mystery of the church that I do not know. I must remind myself that problems within the church do not constitute grounds to abandon it.

The church was not designed by God to be some large monolith with ornate stained glass etchings, distant, forbidding pulpits, and archaic icons adorning the walls. Although nothing is inherently wrong with these things, they are man's constructions, not God's. God's intention for the church can be traced to the Greek word, *ekklesia*, or "a gathering of people." Anytime people were "called out" was a time of *ekklesia*. Nowhere in Scripture does the word *church* refer to a building or do we read of people "going to church."

Chuck Colson, in his wonderful book *The Body*, gives several descriptors of God's intentions for the church. His understanding of the church includes the following:

The church is more than simply a collection of people; it is a new community. Colson says that when we confess Christ, we become part of His called-out people. We are part of a community of the redeemed, the holy nation, and royal priesthood. We naturally want to associate with others who feel called to worship God.

The church belongs to God. The church does not belong to the pastor or the board of elders. It does not belong to the parishioners. Dangerous things happen when anyone begins to assume ownership of the church. Spiritual abuse often occurs when people draw lines and engage in power struggles. The church belongs to God, and we do well to remember that.

The church will triumph. "The gates of hell will not overcome it," Jesus said. He promised that the church would triumph over the forces of sin and evil. Colson reminds us that this is also a commission, that we must stand against evil and fight for justice and righteousness. The church, with all its imperfections, is God's instrument. It was created so that

> God's people will be equipped to do better work for him, building up the church, the body of Christ, to a position of strength and maturity, until finally we all believe alike about our salvation and about our Savior, God's Son, and all become full-grown in the Lord (Ephesians 4:12-13 TLB).

A Ragamuffin Gospel

We can prevent others from exerting excessive control over us in the church—and avoid abuse in all its varied forms—if we will not take ourselves, and perhaps even others, too seriously. In fact, this may be the best remedy to mental anguish of all types.

A reading of Pulitzer Prize winning author Annie Dillard's works, including *Holy the Firm*, reveals her perspective on faith issues. Her writing about religious matters is casual and approachable.

> I only know enough about God to want to worship him, by any means ready at hand. There is an anomalous specificity to all our experience in space, a scandal of particularity, by which God burgeons up or showers down into the shabbiest of occasions, and leaves his creation's dealing with him in the hands of purblind and clumsy amateurs.[6]

Who are we that God should reveal Himself to us at all? she seems to wonder. We are graced, many times each day, with glimpses of His presence, yet we often fail to see Him. Dillard goes on to say,

> A blur of romance clings to our notions of "publicans," "sinners," "the people in the marketplace," as though of course God should reveal himself, if at all, to these simple people, these Sunday school watercolor figures, who are so purely themselves in their tattered robes, who are single in themselves, while we now are various, complex and full at heart.[7]

Dillard's message is clear: We should not take ourselves too seriously, nor should we relinquish power to those who have been ordained.

One particular experience solidified for me the immediate presence of God in our lives. I had spent the weekend at a Catholic renewal center operated by nuns. At first glance, it appeared to be a sober place. The rooms were decorated simply and contained only a bed, bathroom facilities, and a writing table. We ate our meals with the nuns, cafeteria fashion.

I had included as part of my weekend experience a session with a nun whom I was counting on to provide spiritual direction. We sat together in her counseling room and exchanged pleasantries. Eventually, I worked up the courage to ask how she felt God's presence in her life.

"How do I sense God?" she asked incredulously, bouncing out of her chair. She began to dance with delight and pointed wildly out the window. "Look at how God sings with the budding roses. See His delight in the wispy willow. Look at His laughter in the cotton-candy clouds, and hear His voice with the songbirds in chorus. How can you not feel His presence with us?"

I loosened up and laughed with her. "Yes, I see what you mean," I said as I looked out at the gorgeous landscape.

Brennan Manning brought a fresh breeze into the church a number of years ago. His irreverent writings, including *The Ragamuffin Gospel*, caught many of us off guard. He dared to say things that we in the church were thinking. In his introduction to the book he warns "it is not for legalists who would rather surrender control of their souls to rules than run the risk of living in union with Jesus Christ.[8]

In reference to the abuse of power by the church and religious community, Manning says,

> The bending of the mind by the powers of this world has twisted the gospel of grace into religious bondage and distorted the image of God into an eternal, small-minded bookkeeper. The Christian community resembles a Wall Street exchange of works wherein the elite are honored and the ordinary ignored. Love is stifled, freedom shackled, and the self-righteousness fastened. The institutional church has become a wounder of healers rather than a healer of the wounded.[9]

I was touched deeply when I read the account of the prodigal son from Manning's perspective. In fact, I have a habit of rereading it whenever I feel my halo pinching a bit too tightly. In his reading of this famous passage, in which the younger son goes out and squanders his inheritance while the older brother dutifully stays behind to mind the farm, Manning suggests forgiveness precedes repentance when the son realizes his folly and returns home. Many of us want to stop the younger son in his tracks and demand that he explain his delinquent actions before he is permitted to set foot in the dining room. Many of us want an accounting of the lost monies, a humble admission of guilt, and a plea for forgiveness. Certainly, these were the thoughts of the older, responsible brother. But Manning suggests that the father, like our heavenly Father, extracts no such pound of flesh.

When the prodigal son limped home from his licentious life, his motives were questionable. He saw that his father's servants were eating and living better than he and decided to come home. As parents dealing with those circumstances, most of us would be tempted to ask some tough questions. But as Manning says, the most touching verse in the entire Bible may be: "While he was still a long way off, his father saw him and was filled with compassion for him; He ran to his son, threw his arms around him and kissed him" (Luke 15:20). Manning says,

> I am moved that the father didn't cross-examine the boy, bully him, lecture him on ingratitude, or insist on any high motivation. He was so overjoyed at the sight of his son that he ignored all the canons of prudence and parental discretion and simply welcomed him home. The father took him back just as he was.[10]

A New, Old Gospel

Like the prodigal son, most of us are looking for acceptance. We don't know how to ask for it. We may not even understand how badly we need it. We want to be followers of Christ, but do not want to be scolded, shamed, and made to feel guilty when we fail. Fortunately for us, the loving Christ offers the very acceptance we are so desperately seeking. Although pious legalists will always be standing near the door questioning our right to admission, we can smile and say, "The owner of the estate offered me a personal invitation."

The gospel, or "good news," tells us we no longer must suffer condemnation. Because of the blood of Christ, we have been granted forgiveness of sin and life everlasting. We are accepted for who we are. We are not told that we have to change, get it right, become perfect, or show any credentials before receiving His grace. We get it because of God's love for us. Nothing more, nothing less.

The good news is that we have all been invited to the banquet table. Come and dine.

Reflection

How might your tendency to be a people pleaser affect your relationship with your church? Have you compromised your beliefs in order to not rock the boat? Have you represented yourself dishonestly just so you could fit in? Have you ever felt betrayed by your church?

If you answered yes to any of these questions, write down ways that you can practice being more honest with

- yourself

- your pastor

- other people at your church

What are your expectations for your relationship with your church? Are they realistic?

In what ways might your worship communicate acceptance and authenticity?

Chapter Ten

Rethinking Being a Good Christian

*To accept the responsibility of being a child of God
is to accept the best that life has to offer you.*

STELLA TERRILL MANN

I remember her well, though I had to think hard to come up with her name. I knew Ellen only as "the church pianist." She dressed simply, I assume because she did not wish to draw attention to herself. Still, she had a bright complexion, long blond hair, and an engaging smile. I found myself looking at her often, wondering what she did besides play the piano. I never did find out.

Ellen was at the church piano every Sunday morning and evening, week after week, serving without fail. As a musician, I know the importance of song in the worship service. I now appreciate the huge responsibility Ellen took on. I can remember little else about her.

The church pianist. I wonder how she would feel if she thought that was her legacy. Perhaps she would be gratified. After all, countless years of faithful service to one church, one congregation, is noteworthy. She was the quiet voice, the invisible face behind all those hymns. If forced to choose an adjective to describe her, I would select *good*.

I think that she was married because after the songs were sung, as the preacher prepared to deliver his sermon, she quietly slipped back two rows, where a man always reserved a seat for her. They appeared happy.

Her anonymity was typical for many women of that congregation. Ours was a lively church where people spoke their minds, and spontaneous and animated debates often arose, but the central characters were usually men. My dad was at the center of many of the vigorous discussions. Descended from Swedish Lutheran stock, church members usually maintained an accepted degree of decorum unless someone presented an unusually pressing or volatile issue.

Debate was predominately a male activity, though a few women challenged the mold. Jeanette, Erma, and Gladys could be counted on to join the fray. But not Ellen. She seemed content to hide behind the ivory keys. Like most of the other women, she seemed to take comfort in acts of silent service.

Our church honored soft, quiet service. The role delineation was perfectly clear. Women stocked and cleaned the kitchen, folded and stapled the bulletins, and prepared the communion. And, of course, played the piano and organ. (I don't remember one man ever playing the piano for the church.) Men attended to the grounds, seated the parishioners, and received the offering.

Prescribed roles. Assigned duties. Not-so-subtle hints about protocol that let everyone know who would do what and what was considered proper. These rules kept things running smoothly, but they also stifled creativity. The church placed a premium on caretakers, many of whom were practiced people pleasers. Inward, cautious, and uncertain, they looked for ways to blend in. Harmony was one of their hallmarks.

Many women like Ellen perfected the craft of caretaking. They busied themselves with whatever needed to be done, quietly, without expressing an opinion. They served communion. They taught Sunday school. They sang in the choir. But I rarely heard them speak. Even more rarely did I hear them offer an opinion or disagree with a man.

I can't help but smile when I think of the stereotypical church lady portrayed by Dana Carvey on *Saturday Night Live*. Mouth puckered when she spoke, she was critical of anything new or different. Something about Carvey's caricature fit many women in my church.

How many churches today are filled with sweet, cautious, rulebound women, as opposed to assertive, innovative individuals? How many models of vibrant, dynamic women can you recall in your church?

Mixed Messages

Our church offered mixed messages to women. On one hand, women were to use their gifts, just like men, for the good of the whole body. They were equals in the sight of God. They were loved and cherished by God. On the other, our church, like many others, was dominated by male authority. Men served on the elder boards and chaired the committees. They made all the major decisions regarding the church's direction. Women filled positions as deaconesses and secretaries. They could serve in these capacities but were denied leadership roles.

Did Carvey come up with the church lady from his own experience, or is his caricature an accurate portrayal of the model that churches have established for women?

I do not question that the church must maintain biblical order. Scriptural principles provide a framework for leadership in the church. However, I cannot help but wonder how many women, especially in recent decades, have been taught, at least indirectly, to be seen and not heard, and have been treated in much the same way as we treat our children. I cannot help but wonder if the church has inadvertently given women the message that they must "be good," whereas men have been granted more latitude in this arena. Like the larger culture, the church has sometimes told girls to behave and encouraged boys to engage in mischief and challenge boundaries.

What impact have these mixed messages had upon women, and what does this have to do with the issue of pleasing others? Women who have been taught to be quiet, to serve, and to avoid conflict, will be more inclined to blend in and lose their true voices. They will be less likely to speak out, even if they have ideas that are critically important to the well-being of the group. They will be less likely to maximize their gifts when the larger body greatly needs them. They will be inclined to serve others in ways that limit their effectiveness.

Most organizations tend to reinforce conformity and dismiss individuality. Women desiring to actively participate in churches led by men are sure to face an uphill battle. Because men generally deny women positions of leadership, women will still struggle to make their voices heard, in spite of suggestions that those voices are important. This is a challenge that churches must overcome. Women will have to work to show that they can be strong without being aggressive, determined without being controlling, spiritually discerning without being religiously rigid. Churches will have to work even harder to encourage and accept this behavior.

Creativity Lost

The push for conformity in society and in the church is great. Too often, it creates codependency and people-pleasing behavior. It teaches us to be uncomfortable with individuality.

My friend and colleague, Fred, who trims his beard in the car, knows the scorn that individuals suffer. He senses that people question his occupational skills because of his personal quirks. Perhaps you know the feeling as well: You long to be yourself but fear public ridicule. If you have spent much of your life pleasing others, you may have dis-membered many creative parts of yourself. You will need to be deliberate about re-membering them.

Perhaps an artist lives in you that you have forgotten. A singer may be wishing to sing, a writer wishing to write, a speaker wishing to speak. Listen carefully. Can you hear a voice that you have repressed?

Ginny was a church secretary. However, she did not fit the stereotype. She was strong, assertive, and opinionated. She always expressed her opinions with respect for authority, but when she saw something that concerned her, she spoke up about it. She hadn't always been that way. She began her career when she was in her early twenties and had served quietly under the leadership of her first pastor. She dared not question anything he said. He did not tolerate opposing points of view. But when the leadership changed, so did she. Ginny seized the opportunity to explore her abilities. Her new pastor encouraged her to use her skills to the fullest. Even Ginny did not know where this path might lead, but she was encouraged to follow it.

Ginny's role change was subtle. It did not happen overnight. Rather, it changed as she grew older and became more comfortable in her position. The more leadership she took on, the more she was given. Instead of blending in quietly, she spoke up and caused an occasional stir. Not everyone was happy when she discarded the title of secretary and became an administrative assistant. But for Ginny, the name change was significant. She was not being true to herself when she acted as the diminutive, unassuming secretary. She had many gifts, talents, and aspirations that had lain dormant. Her new role as administrative assistant gave her an opportunity to explore her interests in graphic design, writing, and program development.

Both Ginny and the church experienced growing pains. She felt a pressure to fall back into her old role as a soft-spoken, deferential person. She sometimes doubted whether she should voice her opinions at staff meetings. Although she thought that she was being too brash, her pastor assured her that the staff needed to hear her voice.

We need people like Ginny who will speak up even when their voices and opinions are not readily welcomed. These voices offer new perspectives, new insights. They give a broader perspective when we suffer from tunnel vision.

A favorite author of mine, Elizabeth O'Connor, talks about individuality and creativity in her book *Eighth Day of Creation*. She believes, as do I, that we stifle creativity when we ask individuals to conform too rigidly to the rules and regulations of any organization. She says,

> In our society, at the age of five, 90 percent of the population measures "high creativity." By the age of seven, the figure has dropped to 10 percent. And the percentage of adults with high creativity is only 2 percent! Our creativity is destroyed not through the use of outside force, but through criticism, innuendo, subtle psychological means which the "well-trained" child learns to use upon himself! Most of us are our own "brain police."[1]

Called to Be Good

We can all agree that being creative and allowing for individuality, including the free use of spiritual gifts, is a wonderful thing. But we have a huge mountain to scale to fulfill that goal. That mountain is called Being a Good Christian. Or, more simply, Being Good. *Being good* often means conforming to standards imposed on us by friends, family, employers, or the church. It most often translates into conforming and pleasing others so much that we hurt ourselves.

I see a delightful sense of individuality and community in the Scriptures. Just like us, Bible personalities struggled with the nit-picking and backbiting that accompanies relationships. Anytime you are tempted to think that they had a heightened spiritual faith that freed them from the challenges of relationships, look more closely.

Two women had the opportunity to be extremely close friends with Jesus. But they were sisters. (I have three sisters and I can tell you emphatically that nothing is quite like watching three girls or women interacting with one another.) Their brief story in the gospel of Luke gives us an intriguing picture of family life in Jesus' circle.

> As Jesus and his disciples were on their way, he came to a village where a woman named Martha opened her home to him. She had a sister called Mary, who sat at the Lord's feet listening to what he said. But Martha was distracted by all the preparations that had to be made. She came to him and asked, "Lord, don't you care that my sister has left me to do the work by myself? Tell her to help me!"
>
> "Martha, Martha", the Lord answered, "you are worried and upset about many things, but only one thing is needed. Mary has chosen what is better, and it will not be taken away from her" (Luke 10:38-42).

Most of us can readily relate to Martha's busyness. In many ways she is the epitome of one who lost herself in trying to please others. Her mind races as she sees to everything that must be done if this social event is to come off as she desires. Her pace is frenetic, her feelings anxious, and her mood irritable. She assumes the responsibility for getting everything done and is frustrated that her sister will not do more to help her. Martha has an agenda, is fixed on the outcome, and in the process, is scattered and upset. *Whew!* In her I see myself struggling to meet others' expectations as well.

But the story takes an interesting twist. Jesus is not worried about the preparations. Apparently, He is unconcerned about the availability of finger foods. In fact, He appears unsympathetic to Martha's plight. He would rather sit and visit, enjoying an intimate encounter with a great friend. He desires contact, not control.

We can easily criticize Martha. But like her, many of us are caught up in doing rather than being. We struggle to set aside time for the contemplative part of life. We spend too little time reflecting on where we are, where we want to go, and how we might get there. We are too busy maintaining appearances to spend time just "being" with close friends. Somewhere deep within, we have decided to be "good Christians" and to busy ourselves with the appropriate surface behaviors. But the gospel sets us free. It liberates us to *be* rather than *do*.

Losing Yourself

I can relate to Martha. She loses herself in doing. Apparently she felt called to her work. Her perfectionistic inner voices told her,

- Do the best you can.
- Make a good presentation.
- Impress others.
- Work hard.
- Define yourself by how much you accomplish.

As we read their story, we may be too quick to sympathize with Mary and criticize Martha. We might rush in to say one sister was right and the other wrong. Such a dichotomy is overly simplistic. Surely we can see parts of ourselves in both women. Are we not called to care for ourselves while also giving ourselves for Christ's sake?

An aspect of the Christian life that is puzzling to me, especially when considering individuality, is plainly stated in verses like Matthew 10:39: "Whoever finds his life will lose it, and whoever loses

his life for my sake will find it." How do we reconcile the importance of self-sacrifice with the importance of maintaining individuality? This tends to be a struggle for most Christians.

The Scriptures instruct us to live a good life. The writings of
the apostle Paul are replete with admonitions to live a good, a compassionate life, filled with sacrifice.

- Therefore, I urge you, brothers, in view of God's mercy, to offer
  your bodies as living sacrifices, holy and pleasing to God—
  this is your spiritual act of worship (Romans 12:1).

- Do not think of yourself more highly than you ought, but
  rather think of yourself with sober judgment, in accordance
  with the measure of faith God has given you (Romans 12:3).

- Do everything without complaining or arguing, so that you
  may become blameless and pure, children of God (Philippians
  2:14).

- Don't you know that you yourselves are God's temple and that
  God's Spirit lives in you? (1 Corinthians 3:16).

- Though I am free and belong to no man, I make myself a slave
  to everyone, to win as many as possible (1 Corinthians 9:19).

- Do not let any unwholesome talk come out of your mouths,
  but only what is helpful for building others up according to
  their needs (Ephesians 4:29).

Lest we stumble under the weight of all this "goodness," we must
remember that Paul has a singular goal in mind. In all of Paul's writings he clearly affirms that he is not out to please any person but
God alone. He says, "Am I now trying to win the approval of men,
or of God? Or am I trying to please men? If I were still trying to
please men, I would not be a servant of Christ" (Galatians 1:10).
Many of Paul's writings talk about losing himself, *not to others but*

to Christ. This is a man dedicated to promoting the gospel, not to pleasing others.

As we wrestle with the issue of appropriate self-sacrifice and appropriate self-care, we must understand several truths. I refer again to the work of Drs. Townsend and Cloud, and to their book *Boundaries.*[2]

- Setting healthy limits is a way to increase our ability to care about others. Christ modeled self-care by taking time to be with the Father in rest and prayer.

- Selfishness is not good stewardship. Selfishness has to do with a restricted focus on our desires to the exclusion of our responsibility to love others. Having wishes and desires is a God-given trait (Proverbs 13:4), but Townsend and Cloud remind us that "we are to keep them in line with healthy goals and responsibility."

- Meeting our needs is our responsibility. We are to manage our lives, which will mean saying no to people and activities that are hurtful to us. By doing so we are stewarding God's investment in us.

- A lack of boundaries is often a sign of disobedience. "People who have shaky limits are often compliant on the outside, but rebellious and resentful on the inside. They would like to be able to say no, but are afraid."

- We are to give to others but with certain limits. "Each man should give what he has decided to in his heart to give, not reluctantly or under compulsion, for God loves a cheerful giver" (2 Corinthians 9:7). Being forced or induced by guilt to give is not healthy for us or for other people. It is also not God's intent.

- Those people who honor our boundaries and decisions honor us. Conversely, those who only want us to say yes to their requests are often manipulating us to be something they want us to be. Most of our associations should be with people who appreciate our differences and our boundaries.

- Finally, boundaries create healing in relationships. If we say yes when we really want to say no, resentment will result. If we feel manipulated into doing something we would rather not do, we often feel anger and push away. Setting healthy boundaries creates a climate in which relationships will flourish.

Fear of Organized Religion

Most of us struggle to set healthy boundaries in our personal lives. Many of us have difficulty setting healthy boundaries in our relationships with the church as well. When we push away from people or from a church, we may be attempting to set a boundary.

Tragically, we live in a time of fear and disdain for organized religion. Many are steering clear of church in an attempt to cope with negative feelings they picked up as church members. The arguments tend to be very similar:

- I am spiritual, not religious.
- I believe in God but not the rules and regulations of men.
- I have my own personal faith and don't need to share it with anyone.
- I have been hurt by the church, and I'm not going back.
- I don't think God has a list of do's and don'ts for me.
- God is a compassionate, loving God and understands my feelings.
- God is not concerned about church buildings and committees.

Surely you have heard these arguments as well. Maintaining a healthy relationship with the church—just like maintaining healthy relationships with other people—can be a challenge.

I had a conversation with a client recently about this issue. Claudia is 42 years old and undergoing a significant career change. Her transition has created a ripple effect in other areas of her life. With her children grown and gone, she wonders how she will deal with this new phase of her life.

Part of her transition includes reevaluating her feelings about church. She says that she has not been attending because she does not need to hear any more about what she is doing wrong. She has had enough of that. She already feels imperfect; attending church only reinforces that feeling. Gone are the times when she felt embraced and loved by church members who refreshed and nourished her soul. Instead she feels either blatant or subtle shame for never being good enough.

> I went to church for over 25 years of my life. I have been involved as church librarian and Sunday school teacher, and I even served on the evangelism committee. I believe in reaching out and serving others. But gradually, over the years, I got burned out. The more I gave, the more they expected from me. It seemed like the pastor was always saying that I needed to be a better person when I was trying as hard as I could to be good enough. Finally I had to quit because it was starting to depress me. I want to go back, but I will need to find a church that is accepting of where I am and where I don't feel ashamed at how I am trying to live my life.

Kathleen Norris, in her wonderful book *Amazing Grace*, notes that many people are moving away from the church:

> Many say these days that they can't find God in church, in "organized" religion. I don't find that surprising.

> Churches can be as inhospitable as any other institution. What does surprise me is that people will often claim that sitting alone under trees or on a mountaintop is the ultimate religious experience, much superior to being with other people at all. It may be pleasant, if a bit lonely. It may even be private, if you happen to own the mountaintop; otherwise you have to worry about what happens when someone else shows up.[3]

Norris goes on to examine the issue from another important perspective:

> In the rural area where I live, churches are still the only institutions capable of sustaining community ministries such as a food pantry and a domestic violence hotline. But they provide something more, that even the most well-intentioned "social services" cannot replace. It is called salvation, but it begins small, at the local level, in a church that provides a time and space for people to gather to meet a God who has promised to be there. People are encouraged to sing, whether they can or not. And they receive a blessing just for showing up.[4]

Claudia spent several months in counseling exploring her many transitions, including her relationship to the church. I watched and listened as she processed the changes in her life. I watched her search for, and eventually find, a church where she felt loved and accepted. Although she remains wary of becoming too involved, she is slowly exploring ways to express her unique gifts.

Showing Up

Many other people would probably be willing to show up at church and participate in its life if they could be assured that they would not be swallowed up or shunned for being different. If only they could attend and feel that they have become more rather than less. Perhaps that should be one of the church's goals as it wrestles with the feelings of women like Claudia.

Sadly, those who attend church regularly and who are willing to truly engage often feel used. Some leaders estimate that 90 percent of the work performed at churches is done by 10 percent of the people. Of course, any organization will have people who are excited about what is happening and willing to give of themselves. The danger is that too often those who are willing to give don't know how to set healthy boundaries for themselves. For many, especially those with codependent tendencies, seeing a need is tantamount to filling that need. It pains some people to see programs that need direction or people who need help. They feel obligated to step in and rescue them.

A previous pastor of mine, Pastor Jim, was able to set healthy boundaries for himself. He told me, "If a program dies from lack of leadership, then maybe it was supposed to die. Maybe its time was up." On the other hand, if someone had the energy to promote a program, he gave the green light to move ahead. He was not willing, however, to stretch himself in supporting the program. He surmised that if the Lord was truly behind the program, then the necessary folks would show up.

Some people would argue with Jim's approach. They would say that he is callous. After all, if someone came to him and asked for help starting up a street ministry to feed the homeless, how could he possibly say, "Go and be blessed," without being willing to give one iota of his own time? Easy. He knew his talents, gifts, and ministerial responsibilities. He knew that he was not called to be everything to everyone. He spent long hours battling exhaustion and feelings of inadequacy before figuring out that he had to set boundaries on his ministry.

Pastor Jim's wisdom comes from years of experience. He has been a pastor for 25 years, and in that time he has watched at least a dozen colleagues become so exhausted that they left the ministry. He has seen ten times that many parishioners light up with ideas, only to flame out under their burden a short time later. Showing up without being swallowed up is a difficult challenge but one that we must all address and manage.

Koinonia: Sharing in the Community

A good church does not use up its people. It cannot afford to do so. Obviously, if a church uses up its people, it will not be around long.

In the New Testament, the Greek word used for *sharing* was *koinonia*. Paul Lynd Escamilla, in an article titled, "Something Bigger than All of Us," says that this word is rich with meaning—"partnership, community, participation, communion. Literally it means 'sharing with someone in something' and it is used to refer to sharing with God and in Christ, as well as with others."[5]

Koinonia is a beautiful concept. The community experiences honest engagement without enmeshment. No one is used. Escamilla cites several examples of people living in a balanced community of believers.

> In the gospels alone we see the washing of feet, the sharing of bread, the shedding of tears; we see a stranger befriended, a son reconciled to a father, a mother pleading on behalf of her sick daughter; we see Jesus touching blind eyes and withered limbs, enfolding children in his arms, looking a stranger in the eyes and asking for water, charging his closest friend with denial, sweating blood in prayer, caring for his mother from the cross.

When we share such intimate and poignant moments with one another, we sense the magnificence of sharing the bread and cup with one another, the relief of confession, the warmth of shared prayer. Yet we are rarely counseled about the dangers of excessive sharing. These are areas where the church still needs instruction and growth. Even with the inherent dangers of becoming overly entangled with others, the church remains an instrument God uses for His higher purposes. The church is a mystery I will never understand. Even with its rough edges, the church has been ordained by God, and is here to stay.

"No" Has Edges

Edges establish limits by defining where things end. They can be wonderful things, though also sharp and painful at times.

I distinctly remember a conversation with a friend whom I was asking for help. He clearly told me that he had other obligations and was sorry he was unable to lend a hand. I persisted, suggesting that perhaps he could find a way to juggle his other obligations so that he might help me. He then said even more firmly, "What part of *no* don't you understand?"

I admit that I was shaken by the abruptness of his words. There was an edge to them, and I felt it intensely. But those words have stuck with me and cast a light on my tendency to manipulate others for my benefit.

Many of us work to avoid getting ourselves in situations where we might be told no. For example, we dare not raise the ire of a friend for fear of rejection. However, others, like me, push the limit at times. I need to be told no. I suspect all of us need to work on setting limits for ourselves and others. We need practice in saying both yes and no in our relationships.

These words have the power to define us, to make us distinct from others, and to validate our personhood. When you are true to yourself, you may say yes to different things than I would say yes to. You like yellow, I like blue. You like rousing choruses, I like the old hymns. You say yes to bringing children up front during the service, I say send them to children's church. Who is right? Of course, no one is right. Likewise, no one is wrong. We are simply different, thank God.

Sometimes our opinions must have an edge to them just to stand out from the crowd. An edge is often necessary to counteract pressure—from within and without—to conform. Opinions that are strongly held can leave little room for divergent points of view. This was clearly illustrated during the war in Iraq. Though we were allegedly fighting for the Iraqi's freedom, many people on both sides of the debate did not respect other people's own freedom to come to their own conclusions. We definitely experienced tension amid diversity.

Biblical Edges

When we read the Scriptures, we sometimes notice only the passages that encourage us to live in harmony with our neighbors. We especially desire unity. We proudly proclaim that the decision to buy the grand piano was unanimous. Singular points of view can be emotionally stirring, but diversity can also be wonderful. The Scriptures do not teach us to

- live peacefully no matter what the cost
- endure anything for the sake of harmony
- always smile as you persevere
- never say no to a reasonable request for your services
- look good at all costs

This "feel good" spirituality looks nice on the surface, but it is not real. In fact, it does not conform to the instructions provided by the Scriptures. A closer look at God's Word gives quite a different perspective. So different, in fact, that we may squirm when we reflect on our behavior as so-called "good Christians." Consider with me a brief glimpse into the lives of some of the biblical greats.

Daniel and His Assistants

As you may recall, Daniel rose in power and rank to the position of Chief Magistrate to King Nebuchadnezzar. He was given three assistants: Shadrach, Meshach, and Abednego. Along with other Jews, they were forced to bow down to golden statues. But these statues were not their gods. At the risk of death, these three decided to disobey the king's orders. Daniel's assistants were not passive in this matter. They boldly proclaimed their intentions not to bow down to any god but their own and were prepared to pay the price for their convictions.

> Shadrach, Meshach and Abednego replied to the king, "O Nebuchadnezzar, we do not need to defend ourselves before you in this matter. If we are thrown into the blazing furnace, the God we serve is able to save us from it, and he will rescue us from your hand, O king. But even if he does not, we want you to know, O king, that we will not serve your gods or worship the image of gold you have set up" (Daniel 3:16-18).

Nebuchadnezzar was furious. He was not accustomed to insubordination. These willful men would surely pay a steep price for their contrary ideas. He instructed the ovens to be heated to seven times their normal temperature and the three men thrown in to cook. Some of his strongest men bound them and tossed them into the fire. But God prevailed. A short time later the king saw "four men walking around in the fire, unbound and unharmed" (Daniel 3:25).

The story continues with Daniel getting into a bit of a pickle. He too was unwilling to bow down to false idols. Instead of facing the fiery furnace, he was thrown into a den of lions, to be torn limb from limb. But God had other plans, and an angel shut the lions' mouths.

David

David was a mighty warrior, a man's man, and a popular leader. Saul was insanely jealous of David and repeatedly tried to kill him. When David fled from Saul, a band of very rough, strong men joined themselves to him. They were fiercely loyal to David, and when a perfect opportunity for David to kill Saul arose, the men tried to convince David that killing Saul was the Lord's will:

> The men said, "This is the day the LORD spoke of when he said to you, 'I will give your enemy into your hands for you to deal with as you wish...'"

But David was not fooled by the spiritual language. He wasn't swayed by the unanimous opinion of his supporters, and he wasn't intimidated by the strength of these fighters. The men would have pinned their hopes on this opportunity to seize the victory and end the fighting, and David might have feared losing their loyalty by disappointing them. Still, David stated his own opinion clearly and chose a course of action that harmonized with his convictions.

> He said to his men, "The LORD forbid that I should do such a thing to my master, the LORD's anointed, or lift my hand against him; for he is the anointed of the LORD" (1 Samuel 24:4-6).

Nehemiah

Nehemiah provides one of the Old Testament's greatest examples of a leader who was not swayed by other people's opinions. When Nehemiah returned to Jerusalem to rebuild the broken-down wall, the neighboring leaders used every trick in the book to try to stop him. They ridiculed him, intimidated him, lied about him, and planted spies in his camp. When these enemies finally asked for a face-to-face meeting with Nehemiah, his response had plenty of edge to it:

> I am carrying on a great project and cannot go down. Why should the work stop while I leave it and go down to you? (Nehemiah 6:3).

Incredibly, Nehemiah led the people in Jerusalem to complete the reconstruction of the wall in 52 days!

The Blind Man

In John 9, we see an example of fearful people being cowed into submission by abusive spiritual leadership. We also see a delightful alternative.

When Jesus healed a blind man on the Sabbath, the Pharisees missed the wonder of the miracle, missed the evidence that Jesus was the Son of God, and focused on Jesus' lack of appreciation for their interpretation of the law. Instead of celebrating, they convened court and dragged in the man's parents for questioning. Notice that the parents' sole concern was to avoid the Pharisees' displeasure:

> "Is this your son?" they asked. "Is this the one you say was born blind? How is it that now he can see?"
>
> "We know he is our son," the parents answered, "and we know he was born blind. But how he can see now, or who opened his eyes, we don't know. Ask him. He is of age; he will speak for himself."
>
> His parents said this because they were afraid of the Jews, for already the Jews had decided that anyone who acknowledged that Jesus was the Christ would be put out of the synagogue. That was why his parents said, "He is of age; ask him" (John 9:19-23).

How sad! The parents were hardly able to enjoy their son's dramatic healing because they were so afraid to rock the boat! But their son's honest response is a breath of fresh air in a religiously stagnant setting. He starts with a simple, unassuming statement of the facts of his experience. He doesn't try to share any more than he knows, and he keeps focused on what's most important. But when the Pharisees try to coerce him into accepting their prejudiced position, he's not about to back down, and the edge comes out. The Pharisees resort to ridicule and intimidation. In the end, they could not accept the man's presence in their community. But note Jesus' response to the whole situation.

> A second time they summoned the man who had been blind. "Give glory to God," they said. "We know this man is a sinner."
>
> He replied, "Whether he is a sinner or not, I don't know. One thing I do know. I was blind but now I see!"
>
> Then they asked him, "What did he do to you? How did he open your eyes?"
>
> He answered, "I have told you already and you did not listen. Why do you want to hear it again? Do you want to become his disciples, too?"
>
> Then they hurled insults at him and said, "You are this fellow's disciple! We are disciples of Moses! We know that God spoke to Moses, but as for this fellow, we don't even know where he comes from."
>
> The man answered, "Now that is remarkable! You don't know where he comes from, yet he opened my eyes. We know that God does not listen to sinners. He listens to the godly man who does his will. Nobody has ever heard of opening the eyes of a man born blind. If this man were not from God, he could do nothing."
>
> To this they replied, "You were steeped in sin at birth; how dare you lecture us!" And they threw him out.

> Jesus heard that they had thrown him out, and when he found him, he said, "Do you believe in the Son of Man?"
>
> "Who is he, sir?" the man asked. "Tell me so that I may believe in him."
>
> Jesus said, "You have now seen him; in fact, he is the one speaking with you."
>
> Then the man said, "Lord, I believe," and he worshiped him (John 9:24-38).

Paul

In the apostle Paul we see perhaps the greatest rebel, other than Christ, in the New Testament. Paul did not mince words. He was abrupt, abrasive, and even obnoxious at times. He was not your typical citizen-of-the-year candidate. But he was secure in himself and his mission. He was willing to be a fool for his cause (2 Corinthians 12:11). He was willing to say unpopular things so frequently that he spent much of his ministry in prisons and suffered beatings for his beliefs. His passion for Christ burned so hot that it could not be contained.

The list of individuals who stood up for their faith and beliefs could go on and on. Numerous martyrs of the faith stood firm in the face of adversity, each with a story that set them apart with distinction. Few were liked or admired during their lifetimes.

Christians are often uncomfortable with people who exhibit rough edges. They are often surprised when someone says no to what they perceive as a perfectly reasonable request. Some Christians are even shocked when people say no to a request for service, as if they were obligated to accept. But as we have discussed, no is often a responsible response.

John 15 tells the story of a farmer who prunes his vines to create better fruit. So it is with our lives. Saying no to a request may provide more sunlight and air for the fruit that is already growing in our lives.

Redefining Being Good

*Creativeness in the world is,
as it were, the eighth day of creation.*

NICOLAS BERDYAEV

Many of us need to redefine being a good Christian. The Gospels never encourage us to become mousy, soft individuals without opinions. We have inaccurately created this hypothetical individual; the image is not rooted in Scripture. The Scriptures show individuals who are completely human. They possess strength, decisiveness, and character.

Despite all the emphasis on being good, this should never be our first priority in the Christian faith. Rather, our emphasis should be on relating to God and obeying His calling. That unique calling may be hard to ascertain, but we can discover it if we search for it. Elizabeth O'Connor, in her book *Eighth Day of Creation,* says that one role of the church is to promote creativity and the release of gifts. She adds that the church is also to hold us accountable for them so that we can enter into the joy of creating.

Creativity, as I understand it, is all about individuality. Creativity is lost when we try to be the same, to behave the same. O'Connor tells the familiar story of Michelangelo pushing a huge piece of rock down a street.

> A curious neighbor sitting lazily on the porch of his house called to him and inquired why he labored so over an old piece of stone. Michelangelo is reported to have answered, "Because there is an angel in that rock that wants to come out."[6]

While we are awed by Michelangelo's talent, he was simply being Michelangelo. He lived a life true to his calling, just as surely as you and I can live true to ours. Being true to who you are called to be is the best way to avoid exhaustion or burnout. Those that burn out have not been listening to what God has called them to be. Those that become enmeshed with others, or who spend all their time trying to please others, are not attending to their gifts.

O'Connor talks about comparing our gifts with other people's gifts, a common malady of Christians.

> To those of us who keep comparing ourselves with someone else comes that word that it is unimportant how many talents anyone has—two or five. A message that sounds throughout the New Testament is here again in the story of the talents: he who loses his life will find it...This parable says nothing about equality of gifts or equality of distribution, but it does promise the same reward to all—the joy of being a creator..."I will put you in charge of many things. Come and share your master's happiness" (Matthew 25:21).

What a delight to consider that we can enjoy blessings and happiness, things we all desire, as we pursue our calling. We do not find them by being passive and "good" but by expressing our God-given inimitableness. We are not to pursue separateness but individuality. We are to participate in the community of believers but not to the point of enmeshment. The balance is sometimes hard to find, but the journey to discovering our special gifts is sure to bring us peace, joy, and endless surprise.

Reflection

The *koinonia* community is to enjoy honest engagement without enmeshment. We dare to come close to one another, and to God, setting healthy limits, without the fear of being swallowed up. We find intimacy which nourishes the soul. How are you doing in finding that balance?

- With whom are you enjoying replenishing friendships in your church? Are most of your friendships mutually encouraging and strengthening?

- List a few essential components of the assignment God has given you in the church.

- Can you remember a time when you had to put an edge on one of your boundaries? How did the situation turn out?

- Do any of your boundaries need sharper edges right now?

Chapter Eleven

Reclaiming God's Perfect You

You have to live with yourself at least reasonably well before you are able to live with a mate. There must be a certain self-esteem before you can expect that other people will value you highly.

THORDOR REIK

Her offer to let me board in her home was an interesting proposition. I had considered finding a place to stay in the neighboring city since I was commuting between offices, and the hundreds of highway miles were wearing on me. To room with someone, however, unnerved me a bit. Living in someone else's home, even for one night a week, is to be vulnerable. They see into your life, and you see into theirs. Idiosyncrasies were destined to meet and cause a stir.

Sharon had been an excellent editor for my work. Now 75 and long retired from teaching, she still delighted not only in editing but also in teaching me how to write. "Show, don't tell, David," she would say. "Speak with your heart, not your head. Let your readers touch you. Engage with them. Love your readers. Write to them." Her passion was contagious. As I wondered if I could ever truly be a writer, she gently yet firmly nudged me forward.

Occasionally, Sharon chastised me, at times in person, but more often in the margins of my manuscripts. Red ink spilled onto the paper. "You can write better than this, David. Come on. You are repeating yourself. You sound far too clinical. You've lost your heart." When reviewing her critique, she would apologize. "I'm sorry for being so tough with you," she'd say. "I had no right to scold you. Your writing is coming along nicely."

Her words stung. Perhaps I'm not cut out to be a writer, I told myself. People will see through the words and know that I am merely a psychologist masquerading as a writer. Still, she kept insisting that I had a story to tell, and she wanted to make sure I told it.

In the middle of a discussion of one of my projects, Sharon told me she was looking for a boarder.

"Why do you want to rent out a room?" I asked.

"Well, this house is too big for me alone, and I would like a little company. I am lonely since my husband passed away and the children are long gone."

She paused and looked at me with a twinkle in her eye.

"Besides, I could use the extra money."

Her twinkle turned into a full grin.

"Yes, of course. I'll keep it in mind."

I never thought that I would be the one responding to her inquiry. I had a comfortable home and enjoyed my privacy. The thought of compromising that made me anxious. Yet as the weeks and months passed, I considered the benefits of shortening my work day by staying at her home one night each week.

It sounded good, but I remained concerned about a number of things. What would others think? Could I share pieces of my private life with someone like Sharon? Was she a bit too forthright for my sensitive skin? What would I do if I made an agreement and found it to be a mistake? All of these questions, and more, troubled me. I waited, prayed, and considered the proposal. I decided to make the leap. I picked up the phone and called.

"Sharon, I know someone who would like to rent your room one night a week."

"Splendid," she said. "Who is it?"

"Me!"

"Really?" she said, sounding surprised. "I'm delighted."

We spent the next 30 minutes going over the details of our arrangement. I explained which night I would be staying, and we discussed the cost and how I could obtain a set of keys. She described the room, my access to her living room and library, and use of the television. It was all settled.

After having made the agreement, I immediately had second thoughts. Sharon was a great friend, but I knew she spoke her mind directly. Her contract with me was firm, decisive. She knew her boundaries and they had edges. How would I deal with someone who was so sure of herself?

The next two years were a wonderful experience for me. Looking back, I can see that God's hand was guiding me when I debated the prospect of staying in that room. God's work is often clearer in the rearview mirror.

Double-checking the address, I pulled in front of a modest rambler with a large Douglas fir in the middle of the yard. The flower garden burst with lilacs, daffodils, and a gorgeous purple flower she later identified for me. Tentatively I knocked on her door. She greeted me enthusiastically.

"David, I am so glad to see you. Come in. The bed has fresh sheets, and there are fresh flowers on the dresser. Come out to visit after you've put your things away."

I was shaking with adolescent nervousness. I hadn't roomed with anyone for 30 years. I wasn't sure how to behave in a house that was not my own, though she assured me that I was to make myself completely at home.

Sharon offered me tea, which I gladly accepted after a long day at the office. I sat down in one of the stuffed chairs, and we proceeded to talk for the next hour. It was the first of many discussions we had over the next two years. During our time together we

shared many personal struggles and offered each other encouragement and advice as well as compassion. We also practiced setting
boundaries.

As I reflect on our time together, I am thankful for it. I treasure
Sharon for many reasons. She has several qualities about her that
I hold dear. First, she offered me hospitality. She opened not just
her home but her heart as well. She was willing to engage with me.
Additionally, she was deliberate in her decisions, with clear limits
on what was tolerable. She let me know what she appreciated, what
upset her, and what she expected. When I failed to let her know I
would not be coming by one evening, she let me know that she had
worried needlessly and did not appreciate my lack of courtesy.
Finally, Sharon provided me with a model of someone who made
clear, thoughtful decisions to improve her life. She listened to her
heart and was able to arrive at meaningful decisions. She was a
strong, determined, yet sensitive woman.

With all of her foibles, Sharon was a remarkable, lovely woman.
She had done her inner work. She had discovered the lost pieces
of her life and was able to communicate that to me and nurture
my healing process. She encouraged me, through my writing, to
discover parts of me that I had left behind.

Life as Journey

We are all on a journey of discovery, a part of the never-ending
process of becoming the person we are yet to be. I am tempted, as
you may be, to look at certain people I admire and imagine that
they have arrived. I know this is not true, and I am encouraged to
hear that those I consider role models are still trying to find their
way.

Joan Anderson was a woman who had gradually lost parts of
herself to her marriage of 20 years. The mother of two sons, she

found herself growing restless in her relationship. She finally decided to take a sabbatical, a year away from her marriage, home, job, and everything she has been attached to, in an effort to "find herself" again.

The result of her drastic year of departure is a wonderful book, *A Year by the Sea: Thoughts of an Unfinished Woman*. A book by an unfinished woman, dedicated to "my role model and best friend—my wondrously unfinished mother—who continues to evolve and transcend herself."

The book is refreshing, in good part because she does not spend time blaming her husband for her own unhappiness. Joan's story is replete with examples of having lost herself, bit by bit, in an attempt to please others. In the end, she blames no one, not even herself, but she walks away with a clear understanding of the problems that created her dissatisfaction.

This intense time of reflection gave her some insights worth mentioning here because they are true, to some extent, for all of us.

> It's hard for most of the women I know to state what they want, because they have gotten used to wanting only what's available. At least I'm beginning to see what I no longer want: things like making life pleasant for others while forgoing my own desires, writing the script for the last act of our marriage without my husband's participation.[1]

Joan spent much time in anguish before reaching her boiling point. She had spent years imprisoned by a need to be perfect. She tried so hard to be enough in her marriage, her job, and her friendships. She felt obligated to bend over backward for her employer, felt that she had to give more and more to her husband for him to be happy, felt that unless she was the perfect mother to her children she would be a failure. In the end, the price was too high. In order to save herself and the people she loved, she had to loosen her grip on the familiar and head out into uncharted territories.

We are both afraid of and curious about the wild in us. Most of us won't venture into the dark places of our lives, but that doesn't stop us from wondering what is out there. A friend told Joan, "You are never free to do as you please when you stay with the familiar."

Joan finally untethered herself and went searching for what was missing.

Finding Lost Parts

Perhaps you, like Joan, have lost parts of yourself in your family, marriage, church, or work, and you need to recover them. Recovery of anything is a process. The first step involves reflection and time apart to rediscover the parts of you that have been lost. Once discovered, they can be recovered. Someone has said, It's never too late to have a happy childhood. The same can be said of marriage. It's never too late to have a happy marriage. A critical ingredient, however, is determining what needs to be recovered.

As you begin the process of discovering what parts of you have been lost and reclaiming God's perfect you, consider these eight important ingredients. Please keep in mind that when I speak of "God's perfect you" I am not implying that you must become more than you are to be perfect. These steps are simply tools to help you rediscover parts of you that you may have left behind in your journey.

Place

Your environment can either help or hinder your effort to reflect on what is missing in your life. I believe that certain places have the capacity to quiet your spirit and help you to listen more effectively to your heartbeat and the heartbeat of God.

It is not by accident that I live near water. In my island cottage, I am able to reflect on my life and what God intends for me. The water has spiritual significance to me, just as a particular place may be sacred to you. Do you know what kind of place seems to allow you to listen to yourself and God? Is it along an isolated beach, a mountain trail, a luscious garden, a windy outcropping of rocks, a private reading room, a hot bath? Regardless of the locale, we all need to be aware that place can be an important piece of our journey. Knowing this can be a critical first step in understanding what has been lost.

Solitude

Some of you may be frightened at the thought of being alone with no television, no kids, and no phone calls to offer distractions. Solitude is one of the golden treasures our society has nearly lost.

One of my favorite images of Christ is of Him withdrawing from the crowds to be alone in rest, prayer, and companionship with the Father. When I am hectic, harried, and worried, I think about Christ seeking solitude. Do we need more permission to take time to re-create ourselves than what Christ gave to Himself?

Anthony Storr, in his book *Solitude: A Return to the Self,* touts the importance of time alone, indicating "changes of attitude are facilitated by solitude and often by change of environment as well. This is because habitual attitudes and behavior often receive reinforcement from external circumstances."[2]

The psalmist encourages us to be alone with God. "He who dwells in the shelter of the Most High will rest in the shadow of the Almighty. I will say of the LORD, 'He is my refuge and my fortress, my God, in whom I trust' "(Psalm 91:1-2).

Time

Time is a precious commodity, given equally to each of us. Many of us squander our time on things that do not matter. But time spent in prayer and reflection is time well spent because it can reveal so much.

Lionel Fisher, in his delightful book about his six-year sojourn by the sea, *Celebrating Time Alone: Stories of Splendid Solitude*, encourages us to escape. He embraces time and being alone as a recipe for finding yourself. Fisher emphasizes that being alone for a few moments is not enough. We spend our lives taking hurried steps, one after another. As we soften our stride and really see what is around us, we make discoveries. Of his particular journey, he writes:

> Alone at the beach, the epiphanies come fast and furious, partly because I've had so much time to think, partly because I've been searching for the answers for so long...I think solitude does that: it rewards you for taking the time and summoning the courage to face yourself—something you must do alone.[3]

Bernard Berenson, an internationally known art critic, made this comment shortly before he died at age 94: "I would willingly stand at street corners, hat in hand, begging passersby to drop their unused minutes in it."

Space

When I arrive back home after a long day at my office, I am instantly gratified to look out at the water. I have come to expect this kind of reaction from homecoming. You will need to consider where you can create a private space to do the work of reflection. More importantly, you will need to consider how to push some things aside to create this special breathing room.

Reflection

Being alone, in and of itself, will not offer any rewards. Neither will time. However, time alone for reflection can yield a powerful bounty. Reflection and meditation are important to the soul. The soul demands its own space to breathe.

Solomon, the wisest of men, shares these words: "When times are good, be happy; but when times are bad, consider" (Ecclesiastes 7:14). Consider where your life is today and how you got there. Consider what parts of you have been left behind or underdeveloped. Consider that the trials you are facing are part of God's plan for your development.

One aspect of reflection is contemplation. Thomas Merton, in his book *New Seeds of Contemplation*, says this:

> Contemplation is the highest expression of man's intellectual and spiritual life. It is that life itself, fully awake, fully alive, fully aware that it is alive. It is spiritual wonder. It is spontaneous awe at the sacredness of life, of being. It is gratitude for life, for awareness and for being.[4]

Journaling

Journaling is a way of communicating with ourselves. With the freedom to share what is true, without editing our thoughts, we can ferret out what we really think. What may have begun as a frivolous diary in your youth can now become a life-changing internal meditation.

Why is journaling so important to the discovery process? Because there are so few places where we can be utterly honest about how we feel. On the blank pages before us, we can say it just the way it is. We can use whatever language fits the situation without fear of reprisal. Needless to say, the journal needs to be completely private and honored for its extremely personal content.

Intentionality

Intentionality has to do with mind-set. To be intentional is to be intent on mining our deep reaches for treasures. In this case, the deep treasures are thoughts and feelings that are important to us.

They are feelings we have about our lives and about what may be missing from them.

An interesting phenomenon occurs when we are intentional about discovering more about ourselves. The famous psychiatrist C.J. Jung called it *synchronicity*. It involves the purposes of your heart naturally coming together in agreement. Let's say that you are thinking about taking piano lessons when your friend suddenly asks if you have ever thought about playing the piano. Then, two hours later, you see an ad on the grocery bulletin board offering piano lessons. Or perhaps you have wondered about going back to school when there, nestled in the day's stack of mail, is a course catalog from the local community college.

There's no such thing as chance
And what to us seems merest of accident
Springs from the deepest source of destiny.

JOHANN VON SCHILLER[5]

In Paulo Coehlo's rich and popular tale *The Alchemist*, Santiago sets out on a journey as a youth to literally follow his dreams. He meets with a palm reader, the King of Salem, a crystal merchant, and others, to assist him in understanding where his dreams are leading. All he knows is that he must be intentional about following them. He knows that if he follows them he is sure to find his treasure. Though his dream-travels take him through desert storms and through confrontations with robbers and tricksters, he remains relentless. He says goodbye to a fair maiden in order to continue on his journey. Nothing can deter him from his quest. Santiago comes to believe that "when you want something, all the world conspires in helping you to achieve it." We must, however, put one foot in front of the other and resist becoming sidetracked by the purveyors of distraction and fool's gold. We are searching for pure gold.

In his unique and engaging book, *When God Winks*, Squire Rushnell offers another way of explaining the enchanting circumstances of our lives. He says that God is at work, winking at us, offering us nudges throughout each day, to guide us toward our destiny. He renders several promises:

- We are under the influence of a cosmic guidance system (God), and every day we receive little nudges to keep us on our chosen path.

- Tracking the circumstances in our pasts will create an astonishingly lucid account of our lives while providing clarity to the grand possibilities on the road ahead.

- We can learn to harness the power of coincidences to enrich our futures and strengthen our inner convictions that the life paths we have chosen are indeed the right paths for us.

- We will see that coincidences happen for a reason, one of which is to show us that we are not alone.[6]

Accountability

Walk this path of discovery with others who are intentional about rediscovering and reclaiming their lost parts. Without the watchful eye of a caring friend, you can easily become sidetracked or delude yourself into thinking you are on the right trail when you are actually lost. Others who have spent time of their own in meditation and solitude will be able to provide perspective that is critical during these times. Friends who have an intent and purpose similar to yours can be very helpful.

Addiction and Grace

During our journey together, our focus is not only on the missing pieces that have been lost but also on injuries sustained in travel.

These scars and wounds spur us on to seek wholeness and freedom, which is possible in Christ. Christ will meet us at the deepest place of our wounds and provide healing. Why? Because that is the heart of Christ, to come and bring hope and healing to a lost and dying world. Who of us does not want the Great Physician to touch us in our deepest place of hidden hurts? This is accomplished through His grace. No performance is necessary to receive an abundant dose of love and balm for our wounds. This is offered free for the asking. It is, to my way of thinking, too good to be true.

As if that is not enough, we do not have to be perfect to come to Christ and ask for His grace to help us in time of need. He knows our addictions. He knows we have spent too much of our energy trying to be all things to all people. He knows we have bowed down to the idols of possessions, power, and relationships. Too often, we have become overly attached to them, and now they control our lives. Like the cocaine addict or the gambler in hopeless pursuit of the next big win, we too need to break the bonds of our addictions. Like the relationship addict who cannot shake free from seeking the approval of others, we too need to look at how we may seek others' affirmation at our own cost. But how are we to do this?

Cathy shared how she had become enmeshed in all three of these idols: power, possessions, and relationships. After some intense reflection and practice with the tools for self-discovery, she could look critically into her life. She did not like what she saw.

As I have created time and space to meditate and reflect on my life, I realize that I have been overly attached to many things. As I was raising our children I wanted to make sure that they had everything possible. This was to make up for what I felt my parents did not give me. So, whatever the kids needed, they got. They were the best dressed kids at school. And possessions? I worked hard and so did my husband to make sure we drove the newest cars. I loved showing up at the ballpark in a new

SUV and having the kids proud of our accomplishments. It was a far cry from the old Rambler that my mom drove to our games in. I promised myself that I would never allow my kids to be embarrassed.

When it comes to relationships, I worked overtime to make sure that everyone in the church liked me. I was the head of Mothers of Preschoolers, secretary of the PTA, a board member of the women's auxiliary. I washed and ironed my kids' clothes, took care of all my husband's demands, and ignored what I might need. Push, push, push. That was the name of the game. All to cover up my insecurities.

Now I look back and cry. I exhausted myself, and for what? It was all a form of "works Christianity." I wanted to be the best, do more than anyone else, and prove that I was worthwhile. I never took the time to see why I was pushing so hard.

Cathy wept for the lost years of her life; years when she was not really present to her friends, family, or herself. She was so busy proving herself that she never took the time to look deep into her own heart. She grieved for the pain she still felt because she knew that all the "doing" was unproductive. No amount of doing could make her feel worthwhile. No amount of activity or accomplishments could make her feel like somebody. That sense of value and serenity comes from deep within and from a relationship with God in which we understand our true worth in relationship to Him.

Eventually, Cathy began prying the nails out of her attachments to power, possessions, and relationships. Those nails kept her performing when she longed for grace. They were anchored deep and did not come out easily. But she finally heard the creaks as the nails began to loosen. She breathed deeply and felt the joy of breaking away from the things that had dominated her life. Freedom, at last!

Recovering the Lost You

In one way or another, most of us have lost important parts of ourselves along the way. I certainly have. The "salamander dream" I had a few years ago illustrated that poignantly to me.

I had been working excessively; I put in long hours at the office and took little time to enjoy my pastimes of cutting firewood, sailing, and just doing odds and ends around the house. I was in a suit and tie far too often.

In my dream I was living in a decrepit cabin in the woods. I had an overgrown beard and dirty fingernails. Busy sharpening my chain saw and delighted that I could cut wood, I noticed a salamander scurrying across my path. Setting my saw down, I watched the salamander dart under a log. I began to search the hollow fir for the creature. I awakened, sad that I could not find it.

What was the tone and message of my dream? Delight at being scruffy and dirty, in touch with nature and doing some of the things I like the best? Sad that I could not find the salamander that represented something I was searching for?

What did I long for? I wanted more free time to get dirty and cut firewood, something that has always taken me back to wholesome work with the earth. The salamander represented the changing landscape of nature, and how it eluded me. There was so much in my life I was not seeing because of my attachment to power and possessions.

After that dream, I decided to cut back on my practice and free up more time to do things I really enjoy. I decided I needed more time to don my grubbies and get back to nature. The business side was not the only part of me that needed expression. The spiritual side also needed attention.

What dreams do you have repeatedly? What part of you has been left behind that is clamoring for expression? What daydream reminds you of something needing to be done because it is a core part of your personality?

Heartstorming

Another tool that can be used for recovering the lost you is called *heartstorming*. This technique was developed by Robert Wicks and is noted in his book *Touching the Holy*.[7] He suggests four steps to discover gifts you may have left behind. First, he suggests that you write down what you feel your God-given talents are, especially those that you are grateful for and that may have brought joy to you at one time. Two, ask some trusted friends to share what they like about you and feel are your gifts. Three, see if the list has an overriding theme to it. Can it be distilled into a single word or name? Finally, search the Scriptures for a figure that has a theme similar to yours. Who might be your model? Then comes the "heartstorming."

You find a quiet place to relax and breathe deeply. Imagine yourself as the person who has this word, this "name" you have found for yourself. Picture yourself meeting people and doing things during the day as someone who truly has embraced this style of interacting with others. How does this feel to you? Is there a part of this exercise that enlivens you or reminds you of some skill or gift that you have not used in some time? Find a small way to begin to use it again and see how it feels.

There are many other ways to explore missing parts of yourself.

- Spend a weekend at a retreat center in silence, journaling what comes into your mind.

- Indulge yourself in a spa treatment or massage, being aware of new feelings in your body.

- Schedule some time with a spiritual director, sharing the movement of your spiritual life.

- Practice journaling for at least one month, writing whatever comes into your mind and watching for patterns.

- Take a friend to lunch and share visions for your future.

- Practice praying in a new way, such as a walking, guided prayer.

- Practice meditating on one or two verses in the psalms.

- Take a nature walk. Look, listen, and touch some of the plants.

- Spend at least 30 minutes in silence. Notice your breathing and thoughts.

These are just a few of the ways you can listen to your body, mind, and soul, becoming more aware of what you need to reclaim in your life. You will also become aware of what is *not* missing. You will sense what is going well in your life and how, at least in some ways, you may already be following your true calling.

God's View of the Perfect You

We have explored areas in which you may feel less than perfect and examined parts of you that have been left behind. Remember that in God's eyes, you are already perfect. Nothing is left behind. He values every experience, every piece of you. "In all things God works for the good of those who love Him" (Romans 8:28). You don't have to add anything to who you are to be more lovable and acceptable. Isn't that a wonderful thought? You may not be the person you would like to be, but you have God's favor right now. He is in your corner, wanting the very best for you.

Besides rooting for you and wanting the best for you, God delights in your uniqueness. He does not want you to be just like everyone else. Conformity to this world, and those in it, is not one of His desires for you (Romans 12:2). You are one of a kind. Listen to what the psalmist says:

I praise you because I am fearfully and wonderfully made; your works are wonderful, I know that full well. My frame was not hidden from you when I was made in the secret place. When I was woven together in the depths of the earth, your eyes saw my unformed body. All the days ordained for me were written in your book before one of them came to me (Psalm 139:14-16).

Reflect upon some of the other ways that God sees you:

- You are God's child (John 1:12).

- You are Christ's friend (John 15:15).

- You are united with the Lord (1 Corinthians 6:17).

- You are a saint (Ephesians 1:1).

- You have been redeemed and forgiven (Colossians 1:14).

- You are complete in Christ (Colossians 2:10).

God does not want you to compromise who you are or to lose yourself in trying to please others. He is delighted in your individuality and desires that you express your creative gifts, which He knows will bring delight to you as well.

As we near the completion of this book, let's look at some additional practical steps you can take to experience the perfect you.

Living the Perfect You

Perhaps the greatest hallmark of a healthy life, in addition to a mature spiritual faith, is a network of sound, mature relationships with other people. Our relationships are an accurate mirror of how we are doing emotionally. To that end, we must devote time and attention to how we interact with others. This is not to be misinterpreted as a need to please others. We already know this to be a deceptive illusion that will only trap us and make us prisoner of a pattern that will be our undoing. Rather, we must learn to be individuals first, and healthy friends and lovers second.

I am indebted to Pia Melody, a pioneer in the codependency movement, for her seminal work in this field. In her book *Facing Love Addiction,* she shares valuable insights many of us need to realign our relationships. She offers nine characteristics of a healthy relationship that I believe are worth using to evaluate your relationships.[8]

First, she notes that each partner must view the other realistically. She states, "Neither of you minimizes or denies who your partner is, nor hides your own reality from your partner." In this simple explanation you notice the importance of being truthful, asking for what you need, and letting go of the outcome. You recognize the imperfection in others and don't expect them to meet all of your needs. When the occasional boundary violation occurs, you deal with it directly and with aplomb.

Second, each partner takes responsibility for personal growth. Melody suggests that both should be involved in some kind of recovery and growth process. You practice valuing yourself and don't expect that your partner is always going to make you feel good. You practice setting healthy boundaries and encourage your partner to do the same.

Third, each partner takes responsibility for staying in an adult ego state. "Healthy people have mature adult emotions about current happenings, and recognize that their thinking creates corresponding feelings." In the adult ego state, you communicate clearly and avoid acting out childish feelings.

Fourth, each partner must focus on solutions to problems. You recognize that problems are part of living, and you approach them by determining how to resolve issues most efficiently. Because neither person has to be right, you work to find win-win solutions. You do not slip into the easy habit of blaming the other person or telling the other person that they are wrong. You realize that this leads quickly into a negative spin that produces anger and resentment.

In my work with couples I am amazed to see how much energy they use in assigning blame to the other. "Why did you do that?" one might say, or "You should never do those kinds of things." This only creates resentment in others and rarely leads to problem solving.

Fifth, each partner can be intimate and support the other a reasonable amount of time. "When one of you expresses needs and wants, the other can be supportive as often as possible without sacrificing his or her own self-care and without doing the partner's work."

Sixth, make choices in favor of yourself and act out of self-care rather than punishing somebody else for not taking care of you, not respecting you, or for doing harm to you. "As you quit projecting your denied feelings so much, you may come to realize that the other person's action you disliked is often intended to take care of him or her and not designed to do you harm at all."

We often react negatively and codependently when others do not meet our expectations. This is not to say that we should live in isolation from our spouse but that we hold our expectations loosely, and when they are not fulfilled, we take care to avoid taking things personally. Obviously, this is often easier said than done.

Seventh, each partner can negotiate and accept compromise. Here you give up power struggles. You do not need to be right all the time. You avoid playing God, even when giving up is incredibly difficult. You know in your heart that you need not point out every little mistake your partner makes, and doing so certainly does nothing to create good will. When you are operating out of abundance rather than scarcity, compromise doesn't feel as if something is being ripped away.

Eighth, each person is usually able to enjoy their partner despite differences between them. You will be able, with practice, to focus on what you like and enjoy about your partner, even when faced with traits that are not so likeable. The better you become at taking care of yourself, the more comfortable you are with letting your partner be who he or she is.

Ninth, each partner can communicate simply and directly. This gets back to telling the truth in a tactful manner. Each partner takes responsibility for making clear, direct statements concerning needs for intimacy and support. Without blaming your partner for your feelings, you will be able to state how you are feeling at any given moment and to take responsibility for those feelings.

These are powerful tools but only if you are willing to use and apply them. Left in the toolbox, they are of little value. As you review the list, do you see one or two that you would like to begin practicing immediately?

Putting the Pieces Together

Separate but equal. Sharing without blaming. Setting boundaries without being harsh about it. Respecting your partner's right to think differently. Taking care of yourself without losing yourself in caring for others. Saying no. Saying yes. Becoming perfect without being perfectionistic.

Now is the time to put the pieces together and practice the things we have been talking about in this book. These principles have the power to revolutionize troubled lives. Setting healthy boundaries and minimizing codependent actions are extremely powerful tools. If you put the principles into action, you will be well on your way to finding peace in your relationships and in all aspects of your life.

Remind yourself that one step at a time is enough. The lists I have offered can be overwhelming and unrealistic if you expect that you will put each item into practice. But you can try one or two at a time and evaluate the results.

Molly came to me several weeks ago after practicing some of the principles in this book. She was impressed with the results:

I must admit that I am ashamed of how I have been behaving in my marriage. I have been acting in ways that have made Kevin pull away from me. I never really learned how to share my feelings with him and always expected him to read my mind and know what I needed. When he didn't respond I pulled away emotionally and physically. This has hurt both of us and our relationship. I now understand what I need to do to solve this problem.

Tracey shared the following:

I gave too much of my time to the church. I volunteered in the nursery, taught a Sunday school class, worked a full-time job, and came home at night exhausted. Darren kept asking me to slow down, but I was feeding some long-standing self-esteem problems with my excessive activities. Now I am asking for what I need, practicing saying no more often, and he and I are doing better than ever before.

Sandy told me that she has been frustrated with her husband. He had not been responding to her requests for changes. She decided that she could only ask for change and then work on detaching herself from the outcome. She refused to become embroiled with him in struggles about his behavior. She noticed that the more she focused on making her expectations clear, and then stood back and said no more, the more he changed.

Perhaps you can see parts of yourself in each of these women. Most of us recognize tendencies to say yes when we want to say no. We see ourselves feeling guilty for issues that are not our concern. We stretch ourselves to the breaking point in trying to make sure no one is unhappy with us. But we now know that this is not God's plan for our lives. Self-care is not to be confused with being selfish. In fact, self-care is one of the highest forms of maturity.

Each of our stories is slightly different. Your world and my world are not exactly alike. However, most of us have places where we need to be challenged, one step at a time, one moment at a time. With God's help, the journey becomes a little easier.

As you move forward in your emotional and spiritual quest, I hope that this book will serve as a launching pad for you and will point you in a healthier direction.

You are a precious individual. God bless you in your journey.

Reflection

This book is about finding and affirming your true self. It is about rediscovering the wonder of being you. I hope that in your journey through the book you have been encouraged to reclaim your hidden self, your lost self, and perhaps even some undiscovered parts of your self. Take a moment to

- champion the person God has created you to be
- claim each unique trait that makes you an individual
- thank God for your creative gifts and abilities
- listen to the soft voice inside that is calling for recognition— that part of you that dreams for more
- agree with yourself that you will continue the journey of encouraging yourself to grow into all that God wants you to be

Test of Codependence

Instructions: Answer the following true-or-false questions. Using some of the ideas from the book along with this test, you will be able to assess whether you have a problem with pleasing others. These traits of codependence have been adapted from Pia Melody's book *Facing Love Addiction*.[1]

1. I have a tendency to tell other people who they ought to be.
   ☐ True
   ☐ False

2. I allow others to tell me who I should be, and I try to conform to their expectations.
   ☐ True
   ☐ False

3. I tend to be resentful and harbor anger.
   ☐ True
   ☐ False

4. I lose self-esteem when people criticize me.
   ☐ True
   ☐ False

5. I give people power over me by hating them, fearing them, or worshiping them.
   □ True
   □ False

6. I seek excessive admiration and attention.
   □ True
   □ False

7. I have difficulty loving myself, caring for myself, and moderating my activities.
   □ True
   □ False

8. I have physical symptoms associated with stress or emotional problems.
   □ True
   □ False

9. I have had problems with addictions, which I have used to alleviate some of my emotional pain.
   □ True
   □ False

10. Identifying my feelings and needs and sharing them with my mate is very difficult.
    □ True
    □ False

11. I have difficulty letting myself be emotionally vulnerable with my mate.
    □ True
    □ False

Conclusions: If you have answered positively to two or more of these items, you may have some difficulties with codependence that need attention.

Traits of the Transformed Relationship

Recovery does not happen in one single step. It happens over time in a deliberate attempt to change destructive habits. This list of traits of the transformed relationship is described by Sharon Wegsheider-Cruse in her book *Choicemaking*.[1] Read through the list and see which best describes you today. Make some goals concerning where you would like to be.

Transformed Individuals	Untransformed Individuals
Resist conformity	Conform to others
Invent a new lifestyle	Act like victims
Have a creative personality	Are followers
Define their own goals	Have poorly defined goals
Are directed by their inner selves	Are directed by other people
Believe their personal experience	Believe what others believe
Live in the present	Live in the past or future
Accept pain as necessary	Hide from pain
Become whole	Remain fragmented
Have a solid value system	Have contradictory values
Are direct and simple	Are confused and complicated
Are decisive	Are indecisive
Feel free	Feel stuck and powerless

Notes

Chapter 1—Getting Lost Growing Up

1. Virginia Satir, *Peoplemaking* (Palo Alto, CA: Science and Behavior Books, 1972).
2. Terry Kellogg, *Broken Toys, Broken Dreams: Understanding and Healing Codependency, Compulsive Behavior and Family* (Amherst, MA: BRAT Publishing, 1990), xviii.
3. Sharon Wegscheider-Cruse, quoted in Kellogg, *Broken Toys, Broken Dreams*, xviii.
4. Robert Subby, quoted in Kellogg, *Broken Toys, Broken Dreams*, xix.
5. David McKirahan, quoted in Kellogg, *Broken Toys, Broken Dreams*, xix.
6. Kellogg, *Broken Toys, Broken Dreams*, 2.
7. Robert Subby, *Beyond Codependency* (San Francisco: Harper & Row Publishers, 1989), 16.
8. Melody Beattie, *Codependents' Guide to the Twelve Steps* (New York: Pocket Books, 1985).
9. Robert Hemfelt and Paul Warren, *Kids Who Carry Our Pain: Breaking the Cycle of Codependency for the Next Generation* (Nashville, TN: Thomas Nelson Incorporated, 1990), 51.
10. Ibid., 59-60.

Chapter 2—The Pleasing Personality

1. Anne Wilson Schaef, *Co-Dependence: Misunderstood–Mistreated* (San Francisco: Harper & Row Publishers, 1986), 44-63.
2. Ibid., 56.
3. Henri Nouwen, *Lifesigns* (New York: Doubleday, 1989), 39, 65.
4. Melodie Beattie, *Codependents' Guide to the Twelve Steps* (New York: Prentice Hall Press, 1990), 91.
5. Schaef, *Co-Dependence: Misunderstood–Mistreated*, 61.
6. Don Miguel Ruiz, *The Four Agreements* (San Rafael, CA: Amber-Allen Publishing, 1997).
7. Sharon Wegscheider-Cruse, *Choicemaking* (Pomono Beach, FL: Health Communications, 1985), 2-3.

Chapter 3—Getting Lost in Your Marriage and Family

1. Mary Field Belenky, et al., *Women's Ways of Knowing* (New York: Basic Books, 1986), 46.

2. Kay Marie Porterfield, *Coping with Codependency* (New York: Rosen Publishing Group, Inc., 1991), 6.

3. Ibid., 9.

4. Robin Norwood, *Women Who Love Too Much* (New York: Pocket Books, 1985), 143.

5. Melodie Beattie, *Codependents' Guide to the Twelve Steps* (New York: Prentice Hall Press, 1990), 163.

6. Patricia Evans, *Controlling People* (Avon, MA: Adams Media Corporation, 2002), 51-52.

7. Ibid., 54.

8. Henry Cloud and John Townsend, *Boundaries* (Grand Rapids, MI: Zondervan Publishing House, 1992).

Chapter 4—Creating a Healthy Marriage

1. Quoted in Harville Hendrix, *Getting the Love You Want* (New York: HarperCollins Publishers, 1988), 48-49.

2. Susan Peabody, *Addiction to Love* (Berkeley, CA: Celestial Arts, 1994), 37.

3. Kay Marie Porterfield, *Coping with Codependency* (New York: Rosen Publishing Group, Inc., 1991), 118.

4. Larry Crabb, *The Marriage Builder* (Grand Rapids, MI: Zondervan Publishing House, 1982), 20.

5. Henry Cloud and John Townsend, *Boundaries in Marriage* (Grand Rapids, MI: Zondervan Publishing House, 2000), 9.

6. Ibid., 21.

Chapter 5—Controlling Children

1. Robert Hemfelt, et al., *Love Is a Choice Workbook* (Nashville, TN: Thomas Nelson Publishers, 1991), 22.

2. Robin Norwood, *Women Who Love Too Much* (New York: Pocket Books, 1985), 66.

Chapter 6—Creating a Healthy Family

1. Sharon Wegscheider-Cruse, *Another Chance* (Palo Alto, CA: Science and Behavior Books, Inc., 1981), 52.

2. Ibid.

3. Dave Carder, *Secrets of Your Family Tree* (Chicago: Moody Press, 1991), 59.

4. Wegscheider-Cruse, *Another Chance*, 51.

5. Ibid.

6. Robert Hemfelt and Paul Warren, *Kids Who Carry Our Pain: Breaking the Cycle of Codependency for the Next Generation* (Nashville, TN: Thomas Nelson Incorporated, 1990), 33.

Chapter 7—Getting Lost in Friendships and the Workplace

1. Anne Wilson Schaef, *Co-Dependence: Misunderstood–Mistreated* (San Francisco: Harper & Row Publishers, 1986), 53.
2. Robert Hemfelt, et al., *Love Is a Choice* (Nashville, TN: Thomas Nelson Publishers, 1991), 106.
3. Ibid., 115.
4. Ibid., 117.

Chapter 8—Creating Healthy Friendships and Workplace Relationships

1. Jan Yager, *When Friendship Hurts* (New York: Simon & Schuster, 2002), 54.
2. Sandy Sheehy, *Connecting: The Enduring Power of Female Friendship* (New York: William Morrow, 2000), 78.
3. Both quotes are from Sheehy, *Connecting*, 80,85.
4. David Whyte, *Crossing the Unknown Sea* (New York: Riverhead Books, 2001), 60.
5. Fred Rogers, *The World According to Mister Rogers* (New York: Hyperion Books, 2003). The quotes are taken from pages 137, 147, and 184, respectively.

Chapter 9—Controlling Churches

1. Ken Blue, *Healing Spiritual Abuse* (Downers Grove, IL: InterVarsity Press, 1993), 12.
2. David Johnson and Jeff VanVonderen, *The Subtle Power of Spiritual Abuse* (Bloomington, MN: Bethany House Publishers, 1991). See also Spiritual Abuse Recovery Resources, www.spiritualabuse.com.
3. Blue, *Healing Spiritual Abuse*, 26.
4. C.S. Lewis, *Reflections on the Psalms* (New York: Harcourt Brace, 1958), 31-32.
5. Patricia Evans, *Controlling People* (Avon, MA: Adams Media Corporation, 2002), 54.
6. Annie Dillard, *Holy the Firm* (New York: HarperCollins Publishers, 1977), 55.
7. Ibid., 56.
8. Brennan Manning, *The Ragamuffin Gospel* (Portland, OR: Multnomah Press, 1990), 12.
9. Ibid., 14.
10. Ibid., 190.

Chapter 10—Rethinking Being a Good Christian

1. Elizabeth O'Connor, *Eighth Day of Creation* (Waco, TX: Word Books, 1971), 59.
2. Henry Cloud and John Townsend, *Boundaries* (Grand Rapids, MI: Zondervan Publishing House, 1992), 103-105.
3. Kathleen Norris, *Amazing Grace* (New York: Riverhead Books, 1998), 258.

4. Ibid., 261.

5. Paul Lynd Escamilla, "Something Bigger than All of Us," *Weavings*, July/August, 1995, 27.

6. O'Connor, 13.

Chapter 11—Reclaiming God's Perfect You

1. Joan Anderson, *A Year by the Sea: Thoughts of an Unfinished Woman* (New York: Broadway Books, 1999), 66.

2. Anthony Storr, *Solitude: A Return to the Self* (New York: Ballantine Books, 1988), 32.

3. Lionel Fisher, *Celebrating Time Alone: Stories of Splendid Solitude* (Hillsboro, OR: Beyond Words Publishing, 2001), 28.

4. Thomas Merton, *New Seeds of Contemplation* (New York: New Directions Books, 1961), 1.

5. Quoted in Squire Rushnell, *When God Winks* (Hillsboro, OR: Beyond Words Publishing, 2001), 21.

6. Ibid., xxi.

7. Robert Wicks, *Touching the Holy* (Notre Dame, IN: Ave Maria Press, 1992), 85.

8. Pia Melody, *Facing Love Addiction* (New York: HarperCollins Publishers, 1992), 136-141.

Appendix 1—Test of Codependence

1. Pia Melody, *Facing Love Addiction* (New York: HarperCollins Publishers, 1992), 3-5.

Appendix 2—Traits of the Transformed Relationship

1. Sharon Wegscheider-Cruse, *Choicemaking* (Pomono Beach, FL: Health Communications, 1985), 174.

Marriage Intensives

Dr. David Hawkins has developed a unique and powerful ministry to couples who need more than weekly counseling. In a waterfront cottage on beautiful Puget Sound in the Pacific Northwest, Dr. Hawkins works with one couple at a time in Marriage Intensives over three days, breaking unhealthy patterns of conflict while acquiring new, powerful skills that can empower husbands and wives to restore their marriage to the love they once knew.

If you feel stuck in a relationship fraught with conflict and want to make positive changes working with Dr. Hawkins individually or as a couple, please contact him at 360.490.5446 or learn more about his Marriage Intensives at www.YourRelationshipDoctor.com.

Call Dr. Hawkins for professional phone consultations, or schedule him and his wife, Christie, for your next speaking engagement or marriage retreat.

■ ■ ■ ■

The Marriage Recovery Center

All couples experience instability and turmoil at times, but some experience severe crises and need special expertise. Dr. Hawkins, "The Relationship Doctor," opened the Marriage Recovery Center in 2006 to help couples in severe distress. With more than 30 years of clinical experience, Dr. Hawkins will help you and your mate recover from chronic conflict, resentment, and detachment. He will empower you and your mate to regain lost love and affection and restore your relationship to healthy functioning. To learn more about the Marriage Recovery Center, call Dr. Hawkins at 360.490.5446 or visit his website at www.YourRelationshipDoctor@yahoo.com.

Other Great Harvest House Books by Dr. David Hawkins

(To read sample chapters, visit www.harvesthousepublishers.com.)

DEALING WITH THE CRAZYMAKERS IN YOUR LIFE

People who live in chaos and shrug off responsibility can drive you crazy. If you are caught up in a disordered person's life, Dr. Hawkins helps you set boundaries, confront the behavior, and find peace.

NINE CRITICAL MISTAKES MOST COUPLES MAKE

Dr. Hawkins shows that complex relational problems usually spring from nine destructive habits couples fall into, and he offers practical suggestions for changing the way you and your spouse relate to each other.

WHEN THE MAN IN YOUR LIFE CAN'T COMMIT

With empathy and insight, Dr. Hawkins uncovers the telltale signs of commitment failure, why the problem exists, and how you can respond to create a life with the commitment-phobic man you love.

10 LIFESAVERS FOR EVERY COUPLE

Dr. Hawkins shows that times of relational stress are predictable and manageable. They can even lead to positive changes and renewed growth. Packed with biblical wisdom and practical information, this helpful manual affirms the value of marriage and empowers you to grow through your time of crisis.

BREAKING EVERYDAY ADDICTIONS

Addiction is a rapidly growing problem among Christians and non-Christians alike. Even socially acceptable behaviors, such as shopping, eating, working, playing, and exercising, can quietly take over and ruin your life. This enlightening exposé provides the tools you need to allow the healing power of Christ to permeate your life.

NORMAL PEOPLE DO THE CRAZIEST THINGS

Dr. Hawkins offers assurance that the crazy troubles most people experience are very normal *and* redeemable. With biblical leading and a prescription for balanced perspective, he shows you how to work toward health and wholeness as you explore your fears, manage stress, and release shame in having troubles.